C. James

GLOBALISATION
AND
ECONOMIC DEVELOPMENT

GLOBALISATION
AND
ECONOMIC DEVELOPMENT

By
Dr. M. Lakshmi Narasaiah
M.A., Ph.D.

Professor of Economics
Co-ordinator, Dept. of M.B.A. and Commerce
Special Officer
Sri Krishnadevaraya University Post-graduate Centre
Kurnool–518 002
Andhra Pradesh
(India)

D P H

DISCOVERY PUBLISHING HOUSE PVT. LTD.
NEW DELHI-110 002

First Published-2008
Reprinted: 2013
ISBN 978-81-8356-309-3

Published by:

DISCOVERY PUBLISHING HOUSE PVT. LTD.
4831/24, Ansari Road, Prahlad Street,
Darya Ganj, New Delhi-110002 (India)
Phone: 23279245 • Fax: 91-11-23253475
E-mail: dphbooks@rediffmail.com
dphtemp@indiatimes.com
Website: www.discoverypublishinghouse.com

Printed at: Dynamic printers, Delhi

Preface

Many view globalisation as a technology driven global order that has led to an intensification of interconnectedness among nations. This, however, is merely one fact of globalisation, and does not presuppose the ideological homogenisation or the rapid retrenchment of the welfare state that is currently underway.

The dispute over globalisation is not about the intensification of global interconnectedness. Rather, it is over the vision of the global system that globalisation projects. This vision entails a global economic system with identifiable rules of behaviour in trade, finance, taxation, investment policy, intellectual property rights, and currency convertibility, all of which are crafted along neo-liberal principles with minimal governmental regulation. This global system represents a new phase of capitalism which is "more universal, more unchallenged, more pure and more unadulterated than even before".

For many critics, globalisation is essentially an anti-democratic process that excludes the interests of a wide range of groups. But the process is not shaped by market forces alone. It is only made possible by the acquiescence if not active support of governments, especially those in advanced countries.

Governments in developing countries, meanwhile, are often said to be unable to stand up to globalisation without incurring severe costs. The government of South Africa, for example, could be punished by capital flight if it insists on implementing its agenda of social reform. The masses of

South Africa, however, are likely to sustain heavier costs if the government abandons its reforming mandate. Faced with such a dilemma, governments have generally selected the side of capital for a simple reason.

The list of problems caused by globalisation is long. In low-income countries, such as those in Sub-Saharan Africa, where governments have been unable or unwilling to provide their populations with even the most basic protection from the new phase of global capitalism and structural adjustment programmes, the people's plight has been particularly severe.

Opponents of globalisation are addressing genuine problems. But it is uncertain whether they will succeed in reversing globalisation or even in mitigating its adverse impacts. To begin with, many of them are badly organised. Most of them have also rallied around specific issues instead of articulating a comprehensive counter vision. At this point, the counter vision they project appears to be a global system which is not shaped by the narrow interests of capital but which accommodates the interests of diverse social groups. This vision, however, is not yet well developed.

Further more, these opponents have yet to develop viable strategies to constrain globalisation. Some argue for weakening or even abolishing institutions such as the World Bank, the International Monetary Fund, and the World Trade Organisation, which they view as agents of globalisation, it is unclear why business interests and governments would allow this to happen. The relevance of these bodies is only likely to decline if Third World countries, especially middle-income ones, begin to reduce their dependence of them under pressure from their populations.

Yet the main problem faced by these critics is that many of them do not see the relevance of the state. A successful struggle for genuine popular democracy can liberate the state from the grip of corporate and financial interests, turning it into a critical agent for the promotion of broad social interests. Many NGOs rely instead of civil society, though this cannot substitute the state in policymaking. The struggle against globalisation is essentially a struggle for democracy; the state cannot be bypassed, but must be won.

Dr. M. Lakshmi Narasaiah

Contents

❉ ❉ ❉

The Nation-State and Globalisation

The world has changed dramatically. Some of the changes are as yet only dimly understood. We are all going to be confronted with many challenges to the whole concept of government and to the role of the nation-state as we move into the next century.

There are two principal aspects to these changes. Globalisation of the world economies is sharply limiting the independence of action of the nation-state. In addition, we are only just beginning to understand what the existence of one superpower, supreme militarily, financially, means to the evolution of world diplomacy and world politics.

These remarks are directed to the first aspect. Governments are now losing influence. Private enterprise, capitalism, summarised as 'the market', is gaining power. Privatisation is a keyword. Across the political spectrum, liberal conservative and formerly socialist parties have all accepted the downsizing of government, the privatisation of many activities and the reduction of government debt. Governments in crisis in the developed or in the developing world have been left in no doubt about what they should do.

The International Monetary Fund and the World Bank have made it clear that assistance would not be available to countries in distress unless appropriate policies were put in place, and IMF prescriptions often involve substantial and detailed micro-economic reform within a country with considerable hardship for its people.

Meanwhile, competition for international capital has become much more severe. In the early independence years, Commonwealth countries believed they could write their own internal rules about the performance and behaviour of capital. Now those rules have to be rewritten to maximise international attraction. The relationship has to be competitive; the rules have to be friendly to capital. This is a totally different environment from the one in which most Commonwealth countries gained their independence in the immediate post-war years.

The new global organisation of industry has significant consequences for social policy. Many governments would have conducted policies designed to see that workers gained a fair share of the returns of an enterprise. With the globalisation of industry, such policies are no longer possible. Governments now tend to argue for lower wages, for smaller workforces, to maximise the competitiveness of their particular country as a home for global corporations. This has consequences of enhancing the profit share as opposed to the wage share of a particular enterprise.

One direct consequence of these changes is a significantly growing disparity in wealth between rich and poor in all countries worldwide. This may not matter so much if the poor were also becoming better off compared to their own earlier standards but in many cases this is not so. The idea of a living wage is no longer relevant. Workers in some countries are often paid a wage which could not support even the smallest of families. In this day, if that is what the market determines, then that is what must happen.

In today's world, governments must fashion their policies to meet the wishes of the international marketplace. There are fundamental differences from earlier times. The global organisation of industry in which national boundaries become irrelevant is certainly new. Some aspects of information technology can operate much faster and with more devastating effect than the old cable system of the last hundred years. This has led to an explosive growth in financial markets. The volume of money traded each day is huge (and) through modern communications, this finance has great mobility.

We all know enough of markets to know that they favour the powerful, the united and the strong and that markets can overwhelm and destroy smaller players. Sometimes smaller players are entire nations.

Those who suggest that the markets alone must be allowed to determine economic outcomes favour a world in which the large will do much better than the small. So far as countries are concerned, most Commonwealth countries are in the smaller category in a world in which large financial institutions and manufacturing corporations operating globally will dominate trade and commerce.

For most countries, banks and financial institutions, which are part of the culture of that country, will become a matter of the past. Banking services will be American, European, Japanese or perhaps Chinese. The consequences of this market dominance are clear. Corporations need a global spread and many national rules for the good order and conduct of business and commerce will no longer be relevant.

For the world as a whole, the most serious problem is volatility, possibly leading to systematic breakdown. Since the Asian economic problems of 1997, there has been a great deal of discussion about the present system and about changes that need to be made.

For a while it appeared that the United States really was going to move the reform process forward but now the tendency seem to be 'it's all right, we have escaped, leave well enough alone' ...There is a need to reform the system, to establish much tougher international rules for prudential supervision and control. The IMF has demonstrated time and time again that it is not interested in avoiding crises, it is only interested in picking up the pieces after they have occurred. If this is its charter, it certainly needs reviewing. The IMF's present operations are inadequate.

Since governments have seemingly lost significant power to corporations and to financial markets and since they do operate within an increasingly globalised framework, individual governments are not capable of undertaking this task. The task is international and global. Whether it is a reformed IMF or a new institution is a matter for debate.

At their last meeting the Commonwealth Finance Ministers pointed to a number of changes, most of which are desirable, but there was no sense of great urgency, no sense of dynamism. They spoke of a need for new financial market architecture but nobody has tried to spell out what that means.

There are two specific tasks: how to preserve some form of equity and reasonable competition in a globalised market-place and how to establish stability within the financial markets themselves.

The IMF's financial resources should be strengthened as a means of averting crises through the provision of contingency funds. Immediate access to adequate funding can be essential for this purpose if crises are to be avoided. Finding a way to encourage the IMF to help avert crises instead of just reacting to crises after they have occurred is a most important requirement.

In any liquidity arrangement, assisting a country is distress, the IMF should take care not to absolve lenders of their responsibility. In some cases IMF should take care not to absolve lenders of their responsibility. In some cases IMF bailouts have done more to help the lenders than the countries themselves. The lenders need to carry their own risk.

For poor countries, how to protect themselves and advance the welfare of their own people in an unpredictable world is a major challenge and very often a major problem. Apart from moves to establish greater stability designed to avoid systematic breakdown within the world's financial system, there also need to be urgent moves to establish an international body to establish rules for fair trading in a globalised environment. Middle ranking and small countries would have most to gain from such an innovation.

❊ ❊ ❊

Globalisation
A Moral Imperative

Globalisation has become today's buzzword. It has also become a battle ground for two radically opposed groups. There are the anti-globalists, who fear globalisation and stress only its downside, seeking therefore powerful interventions aimed at taming, if not (unwittingly) crippling it. Then there are the "globalist" (a class to which I belong) who celebrate globalisation instead, emphasise its upside, while seeking only to ensure that its few rough edges be handled through appropriate policies that serve to make globalisation yet more attractive.

Many anti-globalists consider the central problem of globalisation to be its amorality, or even its immorality. But these critics have too blanket an approach to globalisation. The word covers a variety of phenomena that characterise an integrating world economy: trade, short-term capital flows, direct foreign investment, immigration, cultural convergence et al. The sins of one of the above cannot be visited upon the virtues of another. Some are benign even when largely unregulated whereas others can be fatal if left wholly to the marketplace.

In particular, the freeing of trade is largely benign: if I exchange some of my toothpaste for some of your toothbrushes, we will both be better off than if we did not trade at all. It would require a wild imagination, and a deranged mind, to think that such freeing of trade leads to debilitating economic crises. Equally, it is illogical to believe, as non-economists who fear globalisation do, that freeing of trade is bad because the freeing of short-term capital flows led to a debilitating financial and economic crises and could do so again. In fact, while there are some obvious simulates between free trade and free capital flows, e.g. that segmentation of markets creates efficiency losses—the economic and political dissimilarities are even more compelling and policy makers cannot ignore them.

Anti-globalist critics are in fact often reacting viscerally to a much larger issue: the victory of capitalism over its arch rival, communism. For campus idealists who have always looked for alternatives to what they conventionally consider to be the greed and lack of social conscience that characterise capitalism, the situation is psychologically intolerable. Some have turned to street theatre, nihilism and the anti-intellectualism that has been manifest in the last few years. The more sophisticated have succumbed to a stereotypical representation of corporation as the evil forces of capitalism that have captured the state, democratic institutions, and even international bodies such as the World Trade Organisation.

What these critics often forget is that certain economic freedoms are basic to prosperity and social well-being under any conditions, and are thus of the highest moral value. Property rights and markets, for instance, provide incentives to produce and allocate resources efficiently, and can in turn strengthen democracy by allowing a means of sustenance outside pervasive government structures. The quality and breadth of democracy can then be enlarged as excluded groups, such as women and the poor, are pulled into literacy, gainful employment and better health through higher public spending or the spread of economic incentives.

Critics nevertheless go on to maintain that the global spread of free markets and free trade is responsible for continuing poverty in poor countries, and for alleged growth in inequality between and within countries. Labour unions in the rich countries also fear that trade in cheap labour-using goods from poor countries.

But I do not think these concerns are well-founded. In India which has almost a quarter of the world's poor, there is good evidence that autarchic and anti-market policies produced abysmally low growth rates at 3.5 per cent annually over a quarter of a century, with a correspondingly negligible impact on poverty has declined. Higher growth rates in turn depend on several factors; but openness to trade and direct investment and a skilful use of markets are definitely and important contributory factor.

As for inequality among nations, it is precisely those countries that embraced integration into the world economy, i.e. the Far Eastern Four and then the ASEAN countries, which raced ahead with dramatic growth rates whereas several countries of Africa, Latin America and Asia that looked inwards failed to deliver growth and also made little dent on poverty.

The evidence on trade and investment impoverishing our workers is also flawed. My own research suggests that the downward pressure on workers' wages due to technical change has been dampened, not magnified, by trade with the poor countries. Research also shows that big corporations use abroad technologies similar to those at home, instead of exploiting lower standards or forcing them yet lower through their financial clout.

One result of these mistaken arguments against globalisation has been an insistent clamour for certain environmental and labour standard to be linked to rules on international trade. But by seeking to create new obstacles to free trade, you undermine the freeing of trade, while mixing up trade with a moral agenda undermines that very moral agenda. It gives other countries the definite impression that you are using ethical rhetoric to mask protectionist self-interest.

The notion that global free trade and investment are responsible for poverty, inequality, lowering of standards and

harming social progress is little short of astonishing. Yet
national politicians and international bureaucrats give it who
think that going along is way of getting along. In denying
the virtues of globalisation, they actually harm the very causes
they profess to embrace.

✳ ✳ ✳

Renewing the State

Many view globalisation as a technology driven global order that has led to an intensification of interconnectedness among nations. This, however, is merely one fact of globalisation, and does not presuppose the ideological homogenisation or the rapid retrenchment of the welfare state that is currently underway.

The dispute over globalisation is not about the intensification of global interconnectedness. Rather, it is over the vision of the global system that globalisation projects. This vision entails a global economic system with identifiable rules of behaviour in trade, finance, taxation, investment policy, intellectual property rights, and currency convertibility, all of which are crafted along neo-liberal principles with minimal governmental regulation. This global system represents a new phase of capitalism which is "more universal, more unchallenged, more pure and more unadulterated than even before".

For many critics, globalisation is essentially an anti-democratic process that excludes the interests of a wide range of groups. But the process is not shaped by market forces alone. It is only made possible by the acquiescence if not active support of governments, especially those in advanced countries.

Governments in developing countries, meanwhile, are often said to be unable to stand up to globalisation without incurring severe costs. The government of South Africa, for example, could be punished by capital flight if it insists on implementing its agenda of social reform. The masses of South Africa, however, are likely to sustain heavier costs if the government abandons its reforming mandate. Faced with such a dilemma, governments have generally selected the side of capital for a simple reason.

The list of problems caused by globalisation is long. In low-income countries, such as those in Sub-Saharan Africa, where governments have been unable or unwilling to provide their populations with even the most basic protection from the new phase of global capitalism and structural adjustment programmes, the people's plight has been particularly severe.

Opponents of globalisation are addressing genuine problems. But it is uncertain whether they will succeed in reversing globalisation or even in mitigating its adverse impacts. To begin with, many of them are badly organised. Most of them have also rallied around specific issues instead of articulating a comprehensive counter vision. At this point, the counter vision they project appears to be a global system which is not shaped by the narrow interests of capital but which accommodates the interests of diverse social groups. This vision, however, is not yet well developed.

Further more, these opponents have yet to develop viable strategies to constrain globalisation. Some argue for weakening or even abolishing institutions such as the World Bank, the International Monetary Fund, and the World Trade Organisation, which they view as agents of globalisation, it is unclear why business interests and governments would allow this to happen. The relevance of these bodies is only likely to decline if Third World countries, especially middle-income ones, begin to reduce their dependence of them under pressure from their populations.

Yet the main problem faced by these critics is that many of them do not see the relevance of the state. A successful struggle for genuine popular democracy can liberate the state from the grip of corporate and financial interests, turning it into a critical agent for the promotion of broad social interests. Many NGOs rely instead of civil society, though this cannot substitute the state in policymaking. The struggle against globalisation is essentially a struggle for democracy; the state cannot be bypassed, but must be won.

The Truth About Global Competition
The Economic Myths Behind Globalisation

Local communities everywhere are on the front lines of what might well be characterised as World War III. It is not the nuclear confrontation between East and West—between the Soviet Union and the United States—that we once feared. It is a very different kind of conflict. There is no clash of competing military forces and the struggle is not defined by national borders. But it does involve an often violent struggle for control of physical resources and territory that is destroying lives and communities at every hand. It is a struggle between the forces and institutions of economic globalisation and the communities that are trying to reclaim control of their economic lives. It is a conflict between competing goals—economic growth to maximize profits for absentee owners versus creating healthy communities that are good places for people to live. It is a competition for the control of markets and resources between global corporations and financial markets on the one hand and locally owned businesses serving local markets on the other.

Two things of fundamental importance to each and everyone of us are now very much at stake:

• Will people and communities control their local resources and economies and be able to set their own goals and priorities based on their own values and aspiration? Or will these decisions be left to global financial markets and corporations that are blind to all values save one—instant financial returns?

- Will the life sustaining resources produced by the regenerative capacities of our planet's ecosystems be equitably shared to provide for the material needs of all of us who inhabit this bountiful planet, as well as for our children and their children unto the seventh generation and beyond? Or will we allow a global economic system that is now functioning on auto-pilot beyond conscious human control to consume and destroy the ecosystem and our social fabric in its insatiable quest for money?

Economists, politicians, corporate spokespersons and the media have for years been touting the benefits of the global economy. They have called on us to support trade agreements such as the North American Free Trade Agreement (NAFTA) and the World Trade Organisation (WTO) to remove the constraints of economic borders and open to everyone the opportunities of growth and prosperity in the global economy. They have promised rich rewards for those workers and communities that become successful global competitors.

Many of the most ardent boosters of economic globalisation met earlier in the year at the annual meeting of the World Economic Forum. This Forum has for years brought together top industrialists and political figures from around the world to advance the proposition that removing tariffs and other restrictions on the free international flow of trade and money is a key to creating new economic opportunity and prosperity. It thus caused quite a stir when the Forum publicly announced that economic globalisation is producing disastrous consequences that threaten the political stability of the Western democracies. Their warning bears close examination for being one of the most honest and accurate assessments of the consequences of economic globalisation yet produced by leading advocates of that process. The observation is that:

- Economic globalisation is causing severe economic dislocation and social instability;

- The technological changes of the past few y~~~ eliminated more jobs than they have create

- The global competition "that is part and parcel of globalisation leads to winner-take-all situations; those who come out on top win big, and the losers lose even bigger;"

- Higher profits no longer mean more job security and better wages. "Globalisation tends to delink the fate of the corporation from the fate of its employees;"

- Unless serious corrective action is taken soon, the backlash could destabilize the Western democracies.

We don't have to go far to find examples of what they are talking about and why people are getting a bit upset as they wake up to the realities of who is winning in the ruthless competition of the global economy. The disparities between the winners and losers in the global competition are becoming more obscene with each passing day.

We are coming to realise that the extravagant promises of the advocates of the global economy are based on a number of myths that have become so deeply embedded in Western industrial culture that we have grown to accept them without examination:

- The myth that growth in GNP is a valid measure of human well-being and progress;

- The myth that free unregulated markets efficiently allocate a society's resources;

- The myth that growth in trade benefits ordinary people;

- The myth that global corporations are benevolent institutions that if freed from governmental interference will provide a clean environment for all and good jobs for the poor;

- The myth that absentee investors create local prosperity.

The Growth Myth

Our measures of growth are deeply flawed in that they are purely measures of activity in the monetised economy.

Expanded use of cigarettes and alcohol increases economic output both as a direct consequence of their consumption and because of the related increase in healthcare needs. The need to clean up oil spills generates economic activity. Gun sales to minors generate economic activity. A divorce generates both lawyers fees and the need to buy or rent and outfit a new home increasing real estate brokerage fees and retail sales. It is now well documented that in number of other countries the quality of living of ordinary people has been declining as aggregate economic output increases.

The growth myth has another serious flaw. Since 1950, the world's economic output has increased 5 to 7 times. That growth has already increased the human burden on the planet's regenerative systems—its soils, air, water, fisheries, and forestry systems—beyond what the planet can sustain. Continuing to press for economic growth beyond the planet's sustainable limits does two things. It accelerates the rate of breakdown of the earth's regenerative systems—as we see so dramatically demonstrated in the case of many ocean fisheries, and it intensifies the competition between rich and poor for the resource base that remains.

This is vividly illustrated by many of the development projects in India many funded with loans from the World Bank and other multilateral development banks—that displace the poor so that the lands and waters on which they depend for their livelihood can be converted to uses that generate higher economic returns—meaning converted to use by people who can pay more than those who are displaced.

The Myth of Free Unregulated Markets

It is almost inherent in the nature of markets that their efficient function depends on the presence of a strong government to set a framework of rules for their operation. We know that free markets create monopolies, which government must break up to maintain the conditions of competition on which market function depends.

We also know that markets only allocate efficiently when prices reflect the full and true costs of production. Yet in the absence of governmental regulation, market incentives persistently push firms to cut corners on safety, pay workers less than a living wages, and dump untreated toxic discharges into a convenient river. In our present competitive context if management does not take such measures, they are likely to be replaced by the owners or bought out by someone with less scruples who will.

The Myth of Free Trade

Many so-called trade agreements, such as the North American Free Trade Agreement (NAFTA) and the World Trade Organisation (WTO) are not really trade agreements at all. They are economic integration agreements intended to guarantee the rights of global corporations to move both goods and investments wherever they wish—free from public interference and accountability. WTO is best described as a bill of rights for global corporations.

The Myth that Economic Globalisation is Inevitable

Many of the people who claim globalisation is a consequence of inevitable historical forces are paid to promote that message by the same global corporations that have invested millions of dollars in advancing the globalisation policy agenda.

The Myth that Corporations are Benevolent Institutions

The corporation is an institutional invention specifically and internationally created to concentrate control over economic resources while shielding those who hold the resulting power from liability for the consequences of its use. The more national economies become integrated into a seamless global economy, the further corporate power extends beyond the reach of any state and the less accountable it becomes to any human interest or institution other than a global financial system that is now best described as a gigantic legal gambling casino.

All over the world people are indeed waking up to the truth about economic globalisation and are taking steps to reclaim and rebuild their local economies. Such communities face basic choices as to how they will divide their efforts between competing for a share of the declining pool of good jobs that global corporations offer and working to create locally owned enterprises that sustainably harvest and process local resources to produce the jobs and the goods and services that local people need to live healthy, happy, and fulfilling lives in balance with the environment.

Our experience with the real consequences of economic globalisation is pointing to many important lessons. One such lesson is that economies should be local, rooting power in the people and communities who realise their well-being depends on the health and vitality of their local eco-system. If it is protectionist to favour local firms and workers who pay local taxes, live by local rules, respect and nurture the local eco-systems, compete fairly in local markets, and contribute to community life—then let us all proudly proclaim ourselves to be protectionist.

Such choices are not isolationist. To the contrary, they create a foundation for creative cooperation with our neighbours—whether they be in the United States or in other countries—to share experience, ideas and technology—and to join in international solidarity in rewriting the rules of the global economy to favour local over global businesses, and to encourage cooperative relations among people and communities. It is our consciousness—our ways of thinking and our sense of membership in a larger community—not our economies—that should be global.

Millions of people are also making an important discovery—that life is about living—not consuming. A life of material sufficiency can be filled with social, cultural, intellectual, and spiritual abundance that place no burden on the planet.

It is time to assume responsibility for creating a new human future of just and sustainable communities freed from the myth that greed, competition, and mindless consumption are paths to individual and collective fulfillment. It will take millions of people around the world—linked together into a powerful political coalition aimed at radical, political and economic-reform to win the war that global capital is waging against us.

✳ ✳ ✳

The Challenges of Globalisation

Globalisation gives rise in some quarters to fears that can lead to suspicion, protectionism, and policies that are ultimately self-destructive. Such fears cannot be allowed to frustrate the great potential of a world in which countries drawing closer together. We believe that countries can face the challenges of globalisation positively, demanding as those challenges may be.

All countries can benefit from full participation in the world's markets, including its financial markets. Protectionist pressures must be resisted and reversed, and the principles of openness and multilaterism promoted by the World Trade Organisation, the IMF, and the World Bank must be honoured. And financial market integration should be seen as a positive force: it offers access of global financial intermediation and a stimulus for more competitive and efficient domestic financial sectors; and it promotes efficiency and growth worldwide.

How encouraging it is, therefore, to see that so many developing countries in transition have been freeing up their trade and exchange systems within the framework of our structural adjustment programmes.

No country can afford to forgo the benefits of integration into global market: the alternative is marginalisation and stagnation. But all countries must take the steps to minimise the associated risks. More than ever before, countries need tightly disciplined macro-economic policies to maintain a stable environment for investors, whether domestic or foreign. And while foreign capital can be a useful—and sometimes vital complement to domestic saving, it is not a substitute for it: domestic saving remains the key to investment and sustainable growth. It is also clear that strong financial institutions are essential to avoid market disturbances at home and to secure an effective defence against external pressures. Competitive banking and financial systems that are sound, well regulated, and properly supervised are indispensable for countries to be able to expose their economies safely to the pressures that can arise in global markets.

The challenges to globalisation therefore add to the need for the developing and transition countries to press ahead with their adjustment and reform efforts. For many, this means creating conditions to attract foreign financing and use it effectively. But a growing number of countries have been facing a different problem: how to cope with large-scale capital inflows. Such inflows, especially when they are easily reversible; provide no grounds for relaxation of adjustment and reform.

They should not be used to finance domestic consumption. In many cases, they call for stronger fiscal discipline; and in some cases, exchange rates should be allowed to take part of the strain. Many developing countries and countries in transition also, of course, need to do more to deepen and widen the role of market forces and to foster more competitive market environments in order to promote transparent and efficient mechanisms for resource allocation.

Is globalisation any less demanding for the industrial· countries? Not at all! It' adds to the urgency of the task of taking full advantage of the current expansion to tackle the deep-rooted problems that are limiting the pace, the quality, and perhaps, the sustainability of their growth.

All has to applaud the increased efforts and commitments to reduce fiscal deficits, but in most cases underlying imbalances remain large and the pace of consolidation too slow. More must be done not only to redress present imbalances but also to meet the growing demands of the future.

Another deep-rooted problem—structural unemployment—must also be tackled sooner, rather than later. Budget laxity and high unemployment tend to feed on each other. While cyclical conditions provide the opportunity, governments must not flinch from the task of improving the functioning of labour markets. How? It is not an easy task: by reforming regulations and policies that impede employment creation and job search.

Monetary stability, macro-economic discipline, sound financial systems, and efficiently working market mechanisms are essential for all countries that embrace globalisation. But they are not sufficient for any. To fight the fears that globalisation sometimes inspires, countries need policies that promote not just economic efficiency, financial stability, and growth but also equity and high quality growth. In too many countries, the quality of growth suffers from widening distributional inequalities related partly to high unemployment but also stagnating wages of unskilled workers. And too many countries continue to suffer from poor governance, corruption and increasing crime.

Of course, economic policy can provide only part of what is needed to rid the world of these blights. But it is a vital part. To promote equity, efficiency, and sustainable growth, governments carry an inescapable responsibility for investment in human capital—through education, healthcare, and well-targeted social safety nets—and also for establishing and maintaining honest and effective systems of public administration, law, order and justice. If these essential services are to be affordable, there is certainly no room for unproductive expenditures—military or otherwise—and wasteful subsidies: they must bear the brunt of fiscal consolidation. So globalisation demands a lot from governments if it is to deliver its promise of stronger and high-quality growth.

REFERENCES

A.K. Sen: *"Pattern of British Enterprises in India: 1854-1914* in *Social and Economic Development,"* Singh and V.B. Singh (eds), New Delhi, 1965, p. 420.

Cottrel, P.L.: *British Overseas Investment in Nineteenth Century,* Macmillan, 1975.

Murphy, Rhoads: *The Outsiders: Western Experience in India and China* (University of Michigan Press, 1977).

Das, Parekh and Parekh: *India Development Report* (1999), Oxford University Press.

Reich, Robert (ed): *The Power of Public Ideas,* Ballinger, Cambridge, Mass USA, 1988.

❋ ❋ ❋

Urbanisation and Globalisation

How we handle globalisation will determine whether our cities and our civilisation will be divided and violent or user-friendly and peaceful. We cannot get a clear picture of urban life in the 21st century, especially in the poor countries of the South, unless we take into account the phenomenon of globalisation, which has already brought dramatic changes make their first appearance. So it is there too that the great upheavals of the next century will take place.

Globalisation gives shape to the "Global Village". The "information era" that it ushers in compresses time and we are now living in a world speeded up as never before. World-wide urbanisation is proceeding at a similar rate and its pace in the poor countries of the South seems terrifying. By 2025, two-thirds of humanity will be living in cities and towns, where the best opportunities in life tend to be.

Globalisation also accentuates a "new urban geography" in both North and South. Islands of rich consumers are springing up in cities amid an ocean of deprived people. More and more unemployed people, immigrants, minorities and the homeless, are pushed into cities by pressure from "market economies". As a result, all urban areas—not just those in the poor countries of the South—will have to deal with growing internal tensions. In New York, for example, the poorest 20 per cent of the population earns 15 times less than the richest 20 per cent.

Cities have always had their smart neighbourhoods and their dangerous areas. But such social and geographical segregation has changed in pace and scale because of the growth in the urban population, the increase in "illegal" migrants and rising uncertainty.

In fact, we have entered a period of historical transition, where discontinuities prevail over adjustment. Radical changes in the nature of production and jobs and the incredible concentration of capital in the hands of the financial sector and speculators weigh much heavier in our lives these days than the state's efforts to adjust and improve the market economy. Segregation in cities has been given a new lease of life whose consequences we do not know. It has reached unprecedented dimensions because of the explosive growth of urban areas.

According to one scenario, things will go badly: The growing pace of globalisation will increase uncertainty about the future. Fear and defence mechanisms will grow among people and institutions, fuelling intolerance, xenophobia and mistrust of everything new or foreign. Urban tensions will manifest themselves with increasing violence, and segregation will sharpen. Public areas will be abandoned and become dangerous no-man's lands, the wretched abode of society's rejects. Cities will lose their original function of being a crossroads for meeting and exchange.

If globalisation also continues to go hand in hand with deregulation of financial markets and an unchanged level of indebtedness of poor countries, the latter will not be able to maintain their urban infrastructures. And if on top of this there is corruption and lack of political will, challenges to the system will increase and violence will grow. Cash-strapped authorities will respond with undemocratic mafias which provide them with funds.

According to a second scenario, everything will be all right: In line with the principle that "everything the state does is public, but the state doesn't control everything that is public," a new social contract will be drawn up between the state, the market, the working population and civil society, including NGOs. Cities will develop a new quality of life by providing citizens with forum for exchange. Jobs will be created in the social sector, in the fields of the environment, education, research, culture and leisure, opening up possibilities for young people.

In the countries of the South, long-term development strategies will be drafted and urban planning practised, taking advantage of the opportunities provided by globalisation but without falling into its traps. Town planning will become part of the political process, and the state will work with the private sector, monitored by institutions of civil society. Adequate housing will be built with the help of micro-credit and controls on the price of building materials. Improved infrastructures will enable marginal areas to become part of the civilised part of the city. Democracy will come up with new ways of governing with the help of networks of involved citizens.

In a transitional scenario, action strategies should fall somewhere between these two extremes. They should include social goals so that in big urban areas a society emerges which is founded on participatory democracy and on "capitalism with a human face" or "market socialism".

But the outlook is less clear than ever. Let us hope the present transition will lead rapidly to a new revival of humanism, whose first signs we are already seeing. This would open up the road to a development which is fair, humane and peaceful.

Globalisation and Knowledge Divide

Globalisation looks very different when it is seen, not from the capitals of the West, but from the cities and villages of the South, where most of humanity lives. Four examples taken from India, illustrate how the paradoxical forces shaping globalisation look when seen from the other side.

Five school children died in a remote village in India after drinking water and powdered milk mixed in a vat that had contained a powerful insecticide. Nobody could read the label of the vat and the children were poisoned. The insecticide in question has been banned in practically every industrialised nation; its sale continues only in places like my country.

Secondly, an important annual event recently took place in North India. Potato growers gather there to exchange the best seeds they have produced in the last year. It is an act of pride for communities to share with other's seeds that will help improve the production of potatoes. A transnational corporation attended the festival and are now working to patent the genes of these traditional foodstuffs in order to sell them as profit.

India's macro-economic indicators are excellent. In the offices of investment bankers, you will be told that India is a great investment opportunity. The situation is not so rosy, however. Thirty per cent of the population have been living below the poverty line for the last so many years. Ten per cent of the population are living below the critical poverty line: their income is insufficient to pay for even minimal nourishment. So much of the workforce is unemployed or under-employed.

A distinguished North American political scientist, Dr. Benjamin Barber, recently pointed out that in the United States democracy had degenerated into bringing one group of rascals in for four years, and then throwing them out and replacing them with another group of rascals for four years. From the perspective of the South, that looks very good! In a context where rascals manipulate elections and stay in power for fifteen or sixteen years, I would appreciate the chance to throw them out through peaceful elections every four years.

Thus, the complaints of the North are often the aspirations of the South. Progress in industrialised nations can be a threat to developing countries.

Ten years ago, in the euphoria of globalisation and the expansion of services and finance that followed the fall of the Berlin Wall, I advanced the idea that we were entering a fractured global order. Globalisation brings us into contact with one another, but it also strengthens profound divisions and fractures in terms of societies and income, and most importantly in our capacity to generate and utilize knowledge. Over the last ten years, the concentration of wealth and power has greatly increased both within and between societies.

There is a real risk of two civilisations emerging, with two ways of viewing and relating to the world: one based on the capacity to generate and utilize knowledge, the other passively receiving knowledge from abroad and deprived of the ability to modify it.

The world now faces the prospect of this Knowledge Divide becoming an unbridgeable abyss. We need the international community to return to the basic principles of international co-operation and introduce the idea that a minimum level of science and technological capability, including access to the internet, is an absolute necessity for developing countries and should be the subject of international solidarity.

This can be achieved. However, contrary to the situation of 20 years ago, national governments are no longer the major players in the game of science and technology. Whether we like it or not, the private sector and the international community of scholars must be invited to the table with governments from the North and South to begin discussing an agenda for the mobilisation of a science and technology for development. United Nations with a mandate for the development of the sciences, has a special role to play in the revitalisation of international co-operation in this field.

High World Trade Growth Vs. Output
WTO Sees Link to Globalisation

World trade in merchandise goods is expected to increase in volume by 8 per cent in 1995 down marginally on the very high 9.5 per cent for 1994. Although the current outlook is for a further modest slowing next year, trade growth will remain above the average of the past decade.

Recent trade growth figures continue to exceed world production growth by a large margin in 1995 probably by a factor of almost three and next year close to double. This persistent pattern relates closely to the "globalisation" of the world economy; a process which, brings far-reaching benefits and which can be promoted through the further development of the multilateral trading system.

The recent growth is as follows:

- a 13 per cent rise pushed the value of world merchandise trade past the $4,000 billion mark for the first time, to $4,090 billion;

- an 8 per cent increase in the value of trade in commercial services, to $1,100 billion, after near stagnation in 1993;

- a 23 per cent increase in the dollar value of merchandise trade in the first six months of 1995 which, allowing for the depreciation of the US dollar, is consistent with a full-year growth in trade volume of 8 per cent.

Globalisation

Over the period from (1950 when the process of trade liberalisation through the early GATT Round got under-way) to 1994, the volume of world merchandise trade increased at an annual rate of slightly more than 6 per cent and world output by close to 4 per cent. Thus, during those 45 years world merchandise trade multiplied 14 times and output 5.5 times. However, the excess of trade growth over output growth varied; from an average of a mere half percentage point in the period 1974-84 to nearly 3.5 percentage points in the most recent 10 years. In fact, the excess during the years since 1990 has been much higher still but it is not yet clear whether or not this represents a permanent shift to a faster rate of increase in the world's trade-to-output ratio.

To the question "will globalisation continue?" In this regard one has to observe two factors—technological change and the evolving strategies of firms and individual investors— impart a natural momentum to global integration. It is government policies which can speed-up, slow down or even reverse progress on global integration. In this context, the role of non-discrimination—in particular, through the "most-favoured-nation" (MFN) clause—is examined.

The MFN Clause

MFN was the centrepiece of a multiplicity of bilateral trade agreements reached in Europe in the second half of the 19th century, a period marked by very low tariffs and rapidly increasing trade. In contrast, the 1920s and the 1930s saw efforts to restore liberal trade through international trade conferences rather than legally-binding commercial treaties based on MFN. The failure of these efforts contributed to the Great Depression and provided some of the roots of military confrontation in 1939. It was only after the War that negotiations established what became the GATT, a multilateral contract consisting of rules and disciplines and based firmly (Article) on MFN treatment.

The GATT system has been a post-war bulwark against a return to the trade chaos of the 1930s. In the 1990s, a disintegration of the globalised international economy on the scale of 1930s is almost unthinkable. In contrast, today "the threat that would be posed by a loss of credibility of the multilateral rules" (now represented by the WTO) would be "a fracturing of the global economy into inward-looking and potentially antagonistic trading blocs".

One can suggest two safeguards against such an eventuality:

* the examination of new ways to ensure that free-trade areas and customs unions remain outward-looking and complement rather than compete with the multilateral trading system; and

* progress in dealing, at the multilateral level, with new issues tied directly to the further evolution of the global economy. These include telecommunications, financial services, environment, competition and investment policies among others.

Progress in dealing with these and other issues at the multilateral level will have a significant impact on the future pace of global integration, both directly and through its impact on the credibility of the multilateral system in influencing the broad spectrum of national trade policies.

❋ ❋ ❋

9

Can Economic Growth Reduce Poverty?
New Findings on Inequality, Economic Growth and Poverty

Many people still think first of 'economic growth' in relation to poverty reduction. Indeed, their correlation is one of the most-discussed issues of combating poverty. The relationship is of great importance because if there is a clear causal dependency, reducing poverty could fundamentally be limited to measures to promote growth. However, if there was low growth or stagnation it would not be possible to reduce poverty decisively. In the opposite case, that of the phenomena having no causal relation, promising measures to reduce poverty could be taken up even without economic growth.

Hardly anyone now explicitly expresses the view that economic development trickles down automatically to the poor. Practical experience has refuted this assumption dating from the early days of development policy in the 1960s. However, a number of studies show development of growth and a decline in poverty running parallel. On the other hand, there are also examples which show that despite high economic growth, poverty is not reduced markedly. The common answer to the question raises is thus: Yes, growth can reduce poverty, but only if additional measures oriented on the poor are taken up. This is often termed pro-poor-growth. But what that means in detail, and whether economic growth as such plays a causal role at all, is not clarified. It is worth taking a look at the arguments on the basis of more recent empirical and theoretical knowledge.

No Direct Causality Between Growth and Poverty Reduction

Among the many indicators of poverty, the income of the poor (income poverty) has the closest relationship to economic growth. An increase in gross domestic product and thus national income could, if other factors come into play be linked with an increase in the per capita income of the poor.

Such a relationship between economic growth and the income of the poor, however, cannot be described as causal, as is asserted implicitly time and again by the statement that growth is a necessary but not sufficient precondition for poverty reduction. Insofar as growth and poverty reduction arise at the same time at the end of a process, they exist alongside each other. It would be almost a tautology to say that the former is the cause or part-cause of the latter. Both express the same thing, namely a change in per capita income as well, and both have similar causes. What matters is recognising what these causes are and what specific factors must come into play so that the income of the poor grows too. Growth as a "prerequisite" or "condition" is then no longer the focus; the priority is asking for specific policies that result in higher incomes for the poor. The detour in thinking about growth is not necessary. Since, however, it is based on similar factors, such as fiscal policy/budget structure, employment policy, combating inflation, and institutional development, economic growth can also emerge if poverty is reduced. The difference of views lies in the fact that under the heading 'poverty reduction' the aim is no longer growth, but a purposeful reduction of poverty.

Therefore, in reverse, successful combating of poverty can be seen as being the cause of growth insofar as activating the capabilities of the poor and using their productive capacity of the poor and using their productive capacity triggers economic drive.

Indirect Causality Between Growth and Poverty Reduction

So even if economic growth fundamentally has no direct causal impact on poverty, growth still can reduce it indirectly. This is the case when due to positive economic development a government has greater revenue and uses the surplus for combating poverty, for example by providing such public goods as education and health services. Also in these cases, however, growth is not a compelling precondition. Even without growth greater government revenue can be achieved for example by more efficient tax collection. And leeway for social welfare spending can be gained by redistributing the budget, such as by cutting military appropriations. Furthermore, an automatic process is not given because the government can also use surplus funds for non-social purposes.

Creation of jobs due to increased economic activity can be another indirect link between economic growth and income poverty, if such a development generates income and reduces poverty. But also in this case I see no compelling causality because, for instance, industrial jobs are not necessarily open to the really poor. In addition, these positive impacts occur to a considerable extent only in the event of labour-intensive development. In many countries, however, economic growth is achieved by capital-intensive production.

Inequality, Growth and Income Poverty

If national incomes, grow, a naïve observer might assume that the income of the poor must also grow along with it. But that would be a statistical fallacy. Even if only the income of the rich grows, this results in macro-economic statistics showing a higher per capita income. What the true conditions are is shown as soon as one divides the population statistically into income groups, such as in fifths, as is usual. It then turns out that the bald figures on average per capita growth can certainly cloak a situation where the income of the richest fifth of the population is growing fast while that of the poorest fifth is stagnating. Despite growth, the gap between the two becomes even wider.

The unequal distribution of income (and of other assets such as property and access to social services), and its connection to poverty reduction and growth has recently returned to the forefront of the debate.

It is obvious that inequality and its changes have direct effects on the poverty situation. Does inequality also have an impact on poverty via its relation to growth, because growth promotes or reduces inequality? Earlier, the predominant view was that rapid growth was linked with at least a temporary increase in inequality, so that a distinct policy of growth initially disadvantaged the poor.

The current dominant view is that growth has no foreseeable effects on inequality and that inequality changes only very slowly, in reverse, however, it is assumed that greater equality is a determinant of growth. According to that view, an indirect relationship between poverty on one side and inequality as a factor dependent upon growth on the other is not given.

That leads to the conclusion that fair distribution has more weight than growth. Fair distribution, however, does not depend upon growth. An appropriate policy is possible at any time, not only after an economic situation has improved. The notion that still shimmers through the debate that "something must be earned first before it can be distributed", is wrong. It is a matter of designing policy and the entire economic process right from the start in such a way that the surplus benefits all including the poor. Important elements of such a policy are, for example, land reform and development of finance systems.

Relationship of Growth to Poverty

According to today's conventional wisdom, income poverty expresses only a part of what poverty means. Not least through the voices of the poor themselves, it has become clear that violation of human dignity and rights, a lack of participation in decisions and exclusion from society, unequal treatment of men and women, and vulnerability are also regarded as poverty. For poverty is caused to a great degree by conflicts of power and interests. Income poverty often is not even seen as the greatest problem.

What relationship do these more far reaching characteristics of poverty have to economic growth? A direct relationship of growth to socially-related aspects such as women's inheritance rights, land rights and exclusion from decisions cannot be seen. Considerable improvements in favour of the poor can be achieved here even without economic growth.

Those who see a strong and causal connection between economic growth and poverty reduction must ask themselves what the prospects are for high growth rates and thus for a decline in poverty. Coupling poverty reduction to economic growth is problematic. If only low growth rates are to be expected.

Another question is whether continuous increases in growth are at all desirable and possible in the medium to long term. In this connection, a difference should perhaps be made between developing countries and industrialised nations. But environmental compatibility and availability of resources set limits to growth for both. Some academics assume that industrialised nations have already reached an inherent limit (stagnation theory) and that the high growth rates of earlier years will not return. Moreover, they add, full employment is no longer achievable due to, among other things, an ongoing increase in productivity, and current unemployment cannot be reduced by customary means. In any case, if growth were to be taken as the major benchmark, the prospects for a radical reduction of income poverty around the world would be modest.

Summing up

Poverty is a complex problem and reducing it depends upon many interconnected factors that is why poverty cannot be attributed to one main cause nor its reduction based on one main strategy. Economic growth is just one strategic element among many others related to poverty reduction. An indirect causal connection between growth and poverty reduction can only be seen because governments will have a greater scope for action due to economic growth, and if they promote labour-intensive development.

Therefore growth's role in poverty reduction must be put into perspective growth cannot be the first thing that comes to mind, nor is it the golden path to reducing poverty. The simplistic theory of economic growth as the main condition obstructs the bigger picture; it clings to the underlying and ongoing belief in the trickle-down effect. Even if there is no growth or for inherent reasons there can be none, there are promising ways to take on the challenge of mass poverty in the developing countries. Up front, governments and bilateral and multilateral donors must have the political will to design economic, financial and social policies so that they are oriented on poverty in a coherent way—the result can also be economic growth.

10

Challenging Traditional Economic Growth

Today, saving the planet is about redefining our economic development models. Stirving towards the fulfilment of basic human rights is an integral part of environmental protection. Without a people-centred development strategy we will fail. Conflicting interests and lack of vision and courage are among the many reasons why it is so hard to meet needs in a world of plenty. We are faced with three major challenges in the 1990s:

- To curb population growth and poverty;

- To search for sustainable production and consumption patterns;

- To promote equity.

Population growth is often associated with poverty. But who causes the major strain on the environment? The 1.2 billion poorest people consume small amounts of the world's resources and contribute little to harmful emissions. They do not cause a heavy burden. The day-to-day struggle for survival of the poorest does, however, undermine their resources, and this causes deaths as population grows beyond the carrying capacity of nature. Here two key elements are essential: to turn from non-renewable to renewable resources, and to minimise use of resources through resource efficiency. We must single out the products and processes that must be phased out and those which may be allowed to expand. Right prices that include the ecological costs will be explored further, together with administrative measures. We are ready to examine the possibilities of using "green tax" reforms to enhance employment and harness pollution and inefficient resources use. By shifting the burden of taxes from labour to environmentally harmful products and processes we might achieve a double benefit.

Transport, waste management, energy and land use are obvious areas that need to be affected by policy changes. Individuals must use their power as green-conscious citizens and shoppers—but, in the end, producers and service providers hold the main key to practical action.

The market must be harnessed to meet people's needs both for present and future generations—starting by making economic policies play by the rules of nature. The World Trade Organisation (WTO) negotiations have provided us with instruments to regulate world trade.

Getting the Prices Right

Car emissions may be cut drastically, but the rapid increase of new cars nullifies the benefits. Even the most ardent technological optimist must admit that we need new priorities or cuts in some products and services. For example, we must improve public transport and resource-efficient cars—and reduce traffic.

Traditional economic growth models fall short of solving the problem of unemployment. Indeed, 'robots' and wasteful resource use replace people. There are great job-creating possibilities in environment-friendly produces and processes. Striving towards equity within and between nations, and within and between generations, is the major challenge of our time.

The fact that 20 per cent of the world's population consumes 80 per cent of the world's resources has too long been seen as mainly an ethical challenge. Ethics are not easily translated into politics, especially when confronted with economic and market realities. As equity gradually becomes a security issue—as it will, if we do not bridge the gaps within and between nations—it will climb to the top of the political agenda.

Many of the main conflict areas of today are battlefields of resource management. These will expand greatly if we do not turn conference statements of good intention into action. The 30 years old commitment of the rich countries to meet the target of 0.7 per cent of GNP in official Development Assistance remains unmet.

Two hundred years of Western-led development optimism reached its peak in the late 1980s. When the Berlin wall fell, the economic growth models of the rich countries had become the universal recipe. But as more and more people aspire to join the ranks of the middle classes, the resulting environmental stress calls for a halt, or a radical change of course.

The call for new patterns of production and consumption challenges our traditional concepts of economic growth and the focus on materialism in our culture. Neither the industrialised nor the poorer countries are strangers to radical process of change, though the reasons for change are shifting. And we are truly facing challenging and conflict-provoking changes.

No nation by itself can solve the problems we face. Pollution knows no frontiers, but comes to us with the winds and waves. We have become more and more interdependent. If we are to attain sustainable development, we must commit ourselves through international agreements, through an international rule of law, through the development of financial mechanisms and through institutional agreements. We must develop means and tools to enhance collective security and mutual interests.

11

Elitist Public, High Growth Rate

The internet is changing the face of journalism. Increasingly media organisations in Asia, Africa and Latin America are posting their publications on the web. Proffessional standards are rising, because international comparision has become possible at the click of the mouse. The internet is serving democratic discourse as civic organisations maintain their own websites.

There's no doubt that many developing countries have very limited access to the web, That is no different in Vietnam, where many villages are still not connected. But the speed of for expansion is astounding. Internet cafes are presently only an urban phenomenon, but they are making access to cyber world increasingly affordable. An hour's surfing cost only about 20 cents, barely twice as much as daily newspaper. And prices are likely to drop further.

Many media houses in the developing countries are already on the net or at least working towards it. Although an internet presence is expensive and doesn't normally add up in economic terms, what matters is the image gained. Many media makers in poorer countries are not even aware that most journalistic websites in OECD states are equally unprofitable. They exist because they have become indispensable from the piont of the view of profile.

- In fact the internet plays a special role in the lives of expatriate communities. They can keep themselves fully informed on current events at home on a daily basis.

This also means that expectations of journalistic reporting are raised. Journalists are now serving on an online leadership accustomed to the professional standards of the advanced countries. This clientele has many different sources of information at its disposal, leaving on the place for reporting, which is strong on rhetoric but weak on facts. Resorting to such means is easier for purely regional publications reaching a public with only limited options for comparison.

Now that the elite classes in developing countries are accessing the major world newspapers on the internet, their demand for quality reporting from journalists at home is raising. Readers know that reporters and commentators in Washington, London or Paris are far more confrontational towards the powers-that-be than is the norm in many poor country capitals with autocratic pasts (or even presents). Both the constant contact with diaspora-country men and the reading of internationally respected newspapers are giving impetus to demands for democratic participation.

• A wide range of arguments suggests that the internet is irrelevant to society in poor countries. These arguments are certainly justified, but they do not ultimately stick. It is certainly a medium for the elite classes, and one which generally requires not only a certain financial power but also knowledge of foreign languages. It is also true that it mostly serves city-dwellers. However, prices for data services and hardware are dropping fast the world over. This results in high growth rates of net usage. Moreover, in countries with poor roads and sales logistics, newspapers too are a mainly urban medium.

Above all, educated, urban middle classes provide the decisive actors in civil organisations. Any tool, which enables them to network effectively, is therefore of great socio-political significance. The internet is particularly relevant here, because legal and economi cal barriers are much lower for suppliers than in the case with conventional media. An adequate internet presence requires much less financial investment than broadcasting a radio programme or printing on a newspaper. Websites of independent organisations are. not only becoming increasingly important sources of information for journalists, but publishing their www-addresses can raise the practical value of conventional media.

All this implies that media makers must up-grade their skills. This involves more than simply learning how to use various computer programmes. They must also come grips with web-based forms of presentation. Readers equipped with a mouse and monitor develop different habits than do newspaper readers in armchairs. Whether text images or sound are required, the best online -.journalism has its own stylistic devices—such as interactive opinion polls. Journalists will increasingly have to master these tools, wherever they may be based.

✳ ✳ ✳

12

Technological Entrepreneurship
The New Force for Economic Growth

Entrepreneurship has emerged as a major new force for change. The dynamic role of modern small business in economic growth has received fresh recognition worldwide. It is essential to promote entrepreneurship and to mobilise the dynamism of the private sector for accelerated national development. An unbridled private sector may not, however, ensure growth with equity. It is the prime responsibility of governments to create policy frameworks that enable businesses to apply technology for competitive advantage and for the well-being of the public.

The Changing Global Environment

As agents of change and progress, entrepreneurs start by identifying a market opportunity and matching this with social or technical innovations. They then proceed to mobilise the resources necessary to drive their business concept to its commercial realisation. The development of a product or service with a high-technology content—never easy anywhere, or at today's rapidly-changing global environment. It calls for restructuring the available technology and business development systems and developing the skills needed by a new breed of "techno-entrepreneurs" to transform innovations into market opportunities at home and abroad. It also requires reorienting the present processes and priorities of technical and economic cooperation among countries.

Amidst the global concerns of environmental preservation, poverty elimination and social development, the practical problems of entrepreneurship are not being properly addressed, even though entrepreneurs will create the bulk of enterprises, jobs and wealth.

A torrent of technology-based goods hits the market every week, ostensibly improving the quality of our lives while simultaneously creating complexity and dislocation. The pace of progress in information technologies, micro-electronics, robotics, new materials, biomedical sciences, space science and other advanced technologies quickens, significantly changing the way we live. The growth of markets for these technologies also proceeds apace.

Further, technological change is taking place today against a background of growing intra-national and international disequilibria. While the transformation from state-centred to market-oriented development is opening up enormous opportunities and options, it has also caused severe short-term hardships. In order to survive and prosper in these changing times, India and its enterprises need enlightened government policies, good technical infrastructure and strong cultural roots.

Traditional production factors are giving way to a new paradigm characterised by new patterns of trade, investment and employment, and by informal networking life-long learning and technological entrepreneurship. The manufacturing sector in India continues to be dominated by food products, textiles, chemicals and other traditional industry, mainly in the public sector. However, change is coming, albeit slowly. State enterprises are being corporatised pending privatisation, and the share of knowledge-based and information-related activities in the marketplace is rising perceptibly. Restructuring policies now place emphasis (often purely rhetorical) on the role of the private sector. The legacy of decades of centrally-planned development is generally inimical to private enterprise. In turn, the private sector has been slow to respond to economic liberalisation in India and generally failed to generate the new employment necessary to absorb new entrants to the labour force.

The regulatory problems of an onerous tax structure and administration, poor access to finance and raw materials, over-regulation of labour and land use, pervasive bureaucracy and restricted markets have been significant barriers to entrepreneurial growth.

Towards Competitive Performance

The imperative of improved performance has serious implications for India if it is to survive, stay abreast and succeed. It calls for national efforts on systemic efficiency and productivity growth, the move from an investment-driven to an innovation-driven economy and sustained higher-order competitiveness; towards enhanced customer satisfaction at home and penetration of selected markets abroad. Concurrently, governments and business have to address such intractable problems as poverty, corruption and the degradation of the environment.

Creating New Technology-based Ventures

Starting a new business in India is a hazardous task. Problems are compounded when the venture is technology-based:

- Capital requirements are generally larger, while traditional banks are ill-equipped to process the perceived risk. Venture capital generally only becomes an option when the venture has documented the merits of its management, market and innovation;

- Knowledge-based ventures can benefit from linkages to sources of knowledge—e.g. the technical university or research lab. Such mentoring needs to be cultivated;

- Techno-entrepreneurs often have technical skills but usually lack the business management and marketing skills necessary for success. These need to be supplemented;

- In fields where technology is changing rapidly, it is often advantageous to make technology-acquisition arrangements. Sourcing such innovations, negotiating technology licensing agreements and protecting the intellectual property itself require special skills;

- Knowledge-based innovations are inherently more risky than others. The management of this unique risk requires assessment techniques and vision;

- Technology-based ventures often have social and environmental implications, which need to be managed carefully;

- Penetrating a competitive market requires good market intelligence, a good strategic plan and good luck.

Special Characteristics of "Techno-entrepreneurs"

The popular misconceptions are that techno-entrepreneurs are born, not made; that they take risks with other people's money and fail more often than they successed. In fact, entrepreneur skills can be identified and developed. The entrepreneur is typically an innovator who formulates new solutions to existing problems, mobilises resources and stimulates others to participate in his or her team. These aptitudes develop over time, often starting in childhood, as the person faces new challenges and learns from failure.

Entrepreneurial opportunities can be found in every industrialising country, community and family. Principal sources of entrepreneurs for knowledge-based ventures are often the university and government research laboratories, the large industrial and military establishments and professional service firms. Some motivations of the entrepreneur are the need to: be independent; create value; contribute to society; earn recognition; become rich or; quite often, simply not to be unemployed. Value-adding ventures with good growth potential can best be developed in an open market and in a culture which supports risk-taking.

The techno-entrepreneur anywhere has the challenge of moving a concept through the prototype and production phases towards creation of a product which meets market needs at a price consistent with the value created and with the ability of customers to pay.

Equally important, the market itself has to be developed and sustained. It is not enough to be first with a better mousetrap if one does not have the skills to educate and reach potential buyers and to set the market standard.

Hence one has to distinguish between innovators and inventors. The inventor is typically a creative person in a quest for knowledge or for producing new products, without determining in advance whether a real market exists for his or her inventions. On the other hand, the innovator draws on existing knowledge and the talents of others to develop or adapt a product or service at a volume and cost that can capture a significant portion of an identified market. The flexibility and creativity of a small entrepreneurial techno-venture may lead to more incremental and break-through innovations than can be generated by larger-sized firms in many sectors.

The pace and pattern of India's economic development now depend in large measure on its technical resource base. In this context, the key determinants are the skills to apply technology for enhanced competitiveness, as well as to create techbased ventures. Techno-entrepreneurs have to be supported by appropriate national structures and international linkages if they are to survive and flourish in an intensely competitive world.

13

Migration and Development

Migration and development is a growing area of interest. There has been much debate on the negative impacts of migration on development and vice-versa. On the one hand, it is argued that underdevelopment is a cause of migration, and on the other that migration causes developing countries to lose their highly skilled nationals.

While there is a measure of truth in each of these assertions, properly managed international migration holds enormous potential for the development of countries. Remittances have become a prominent source of external funding for developing countries that surpass official development assistance. In 2005, over US $ 100 billion were sent home in remittances by migrants, helping to sustain the economies of many developing countries. The total amount of resource remitted may even be two or three times higher, since a large number of transactions are carried out through informal channels. Migration can thus contribute to the reduction of poverty at the local and national level, and to a reduction in the economic vulnerability of developing countries.

Migration may be detrimental to the community of origin if the labour market is depleted by the departure of its most productive and/or qualified members ("brain drain"). However, migrants who have developed and improved their skills abroad can be actors of the "brain gain" by transferring and infusing knowledge, skills and technology into their countries, of origin.

In addition, remittances sent home by migrants can be used to sustain development. The challenge is to develop mechanisms to mitigate as much as possible the negative effects of "brain drain" and to encourage the return of qualified nationals resulting "brain gain"

It should also be noted that in a globalised world, migration is increasingly circular. While many migrants still make a permanent move with their families, an increasing proportion of migratory movements are temporary in nature. Increasingly, countries of origin expect migrants to maintain financial, cultural and sometimes political links with their home country, which may be difficult to reconcile with the expectation for migrants to integrate, on the part of the host country.

In order to benefit from remittances, skills transfer and investment opportunities, it is necessary to create and maintain links between migrants and their potential by encouraging them to contribute human and financial capital to the development of their home communities.

Through advances in communications technology and the decline in travel costs, globalisation has made it easier for migrants to stay in contact with their country of origin and to establish lasting links with diasporas and transnational networks.

In the past, states and the international community formulated and implemented separate policies on poverty reduction, globalisation, security, refugees and migration, with sometimes different or even conflicting objectives.

Better results can be achieved by considering the close interrelationship between migration and development on national and international levels through coherent and coordinated development and migration polices, and between humanitarian assistance and development assistance. Migration polices dealing with the migration-development nexus include facilitating voluntary return and reintegration, either temporary or permanent, particularly of the highly skilled. Other policies address the transfer of remittances, the reduction of transfer costs and investment in the country of origin by diasporas and returning migrants.

It is also necessary to promote and enhance dialogue and cooperation and the national level between different government agencies as well as at the international level. The aim is to ensure that migration contributes to sustainable development, and that in turn development endeavours to contribute to the management of migration.

In recent years, migration has been making its way steadily to the top of the international agenda, and now calls insistently and urgently for the attention of all governments, regardless of their past involvement or interest in the management of migratory processes.

Migratory flows today are more diverse and complex, with more temporary and circular migration. World demographics, economic, political and social trends mean that governments and societies will need to put more emphasis on migration management in all of its dimensions.

If properly managed, migration can be beneficial for all states and societies. If left unmanaged, it can lead to the exploitation of individual migrations, particularly through human trafficking and migrant smuggling, and be a source of social tension, insecurity and bad relations between nations.

Effective management is required to maximise the positive effects of migration and minimise potentially negative consequences. It is essential to establish orderly and safe migration opportunities while ensuring respect for the integrity of national, sovereign borders. Migration management strategies need to result in the implementation of policies; laws and regulations that take into account the rights and obligations of migrations as well as the social and economic interests of nations and responsibilities of governments.

Over the past decades governments have tended to focus on isolated elements of migration and have thus developed ad-hoc strategies to protect their interests. For some, labour migration needs have predominated, for others asylum has been the main concern. However, to be effective, migration management strategies need to address migration in a comprehensive manner. Governments over the past decades have tended to focus on isolated elements of migration. The challenge today is to shift from an isolate and largely in effective focus to more meaningful, constructive and comprehensive approaches.

At the same time, it is necessary to identify, define and address the fundamental policy issues in·the migration debates. This is a tall. assignment, since the migratory landscape is complex and rapidly evolving, with challenges emerging at every step of the way.

Most governments are just beginning to develop coherent and comprehensive migration management strategies. There is still a need to better understand migration interests and priorities and to develop a common migration language. Regular dialogue between governments that allows an exchange of experience and the development of new initiatives and approaches to migration management is therefore essential.

✳ ✳ ✳

14

Economics and Sustainable Development

Economists and ecologists were once seen as enemies: environmental protection, it was thought, could only be achieved at the expense of economic growth. The misconception persists at the extremes among both the most fundamentalist Greens and the most ideological free marketers. But increasingly it is now being recognised that development and care for the environment go hand in hand. This interdependence is coalescing in the new and necessary discipline of environmental economics.

Conventional economics patterns have often assumed that growth and technical progress will nullify all resource and environmental limits. Environmental economics recognises that the world's natural capital underpins all development, and that it is rapidly becoming scarcer as human demands exceed the globe's long-term carrying capacity. Government of India has introduced environmental measures over the last two decades, but need to move further towards integrating them into economic policies. There can be no real sustainable development unless environment and development policies are integrated at the very beginning of the decision-making process.

Quantifying the Environmental Cost

One of the first steps is to work out the true costs of polluting and depleting the world's natural resources, such as its soil, air and water, the climate and the ozone layer. These have often been regarded as free goods, and it was believed that the world has an infinite capacity to absorb the effects of human activities. Environmental economists, recognising that the social and economic costs of degradation are very great, are trying to quantify them. They say that this will make possible better use of such tools as cost-benefit analysis, environmental impact assessment and risk assessment—and the production of national income accounts which reflect the depletion an degradation of natural resources. As these costs are identified and quantified, economic policy can increasingly be developed with sustainable development as the primary objective. Achieving sustainable development requires industrialised and developing countries to make dramatic changes in national and international policies based on a global partnership. The greenhouse effect, the destruction of the ozone layer, the extinction of species and contamination of the oceans, and other environmental problems, affect us all, no matter which corner of the globe we inhabit.

The first and essential step in overcoming a difficulty is to recognise it and understand it. Concern over the difficulties related to sustainability has led scientists and national and international institutions to study the concept and suggest ways of meeting its many requirements. Indicators have been established to measure pollution levels, soil erosion, salinisation, deforestation and a host of environmental problems. Evaluating the impact of such natural resource-use on ecosystems is a major step towards finding the necessary solutions.

For example, it has become clear, on a macro-economic level, that national accounting systems fail to reflect these effects adequately, Deterioration of the world's rivers, land degradation, air pollution and contamination of the seas are not taken into consideration. Inadequate accounting distorts reality and gives a false idea of the true consequences of growth and production.

On a micro-economic level, much is being done to redefine production costs. Incorporating the cost of waste management and internalising negative external impacts within production prices are beneficial aspects of the economics of sustainability.

Steps are being taken to evaluate public and commonly held assets and to put a price on them, even though they may not be subject to market forces. These are only in the earliest stage but they will allow for more accurate evaluation of the world's natural capital. Fiscal, market, quota and other instruments are being developed to enforce change in the way in which certain resources are used. Examples include markets for transferable emission quotas or compensatory taxation mechanisms designed to ensure that economic forces act to reduce greenhouse gas emissions. Efforts at impact analysis—and in a general sense, cost-benefit analysis—permit rough estimations of the impact that projects might have on ecosystems.

Long-term Repercussions

These instruments carry significant limitations but they are important nevertheless because they attempt to quantify impacts on the natural world and to achieve a more rational use of natural resources. The development of such instruments and evaluation techniques will have significant repercussions in the formulation of sustainable long-term policies. But we must bear in mind that sustainability is not just an economic issue: it is also a political and cultural one.

The concept of sustainability demands as alternative view point in which humankind and the natural world are perceived as a unit—as different yet mutually sustaining aspects of a whole. This perception is not incompatible with progress. It does not renounce development. It simply seeks to affirm life and refuses to discriminate between the means and the end. It understands that happiness cannot be achieved by destructive means. The questions of how to produce and how to consume therefore become extremely important. Neither should be at the expense of the future or of the natural world. Efficiency is not limited to the links between investment, products and prices: it must address the rational use of resources, including environmental and cultural consequences, both in the long- and the short-term.

Very considerable adjustments must be made in the interests of sustainable development. They demand a reassessment of all our activities which cannot, logically, be done overnight. It is a long and continuous process, characterised by steadfastness and compromise.

✳ ✳ ✳

15

The Dematerialisation of the World Economy

The first Industrial Revolution marked the transition from robber-and-plunder colonialism to the systematic development of the "overseas" territories in the framework of an international division of labour between raw material suppliers and manufacturers of finished goods. There was an "historic integration" of the colonised areas in the development of their parent-states. What will the third Industrial Revolution do for the Third World ? Will it now come to an "historic separation" ?

The end of the East-West conflict was reason enough to talk about a radical change in world politics. But at the same time an upheaval in the world economy is taking place that possibly will have even wider impacts. As a reference point for the following thoughts, three dimensions of this change are pointed out:

1. the upgrading of processing information rather than materials as object of economic activity (technological dimension);

2. the evolvement of global communication networks (socio-cultural dimension);

3. the change of the nature of work (socio-economic dimension).

All three dimensions can be summarised under the buzzphrase "tertialisation of the world economy."

In that respect, talk of the "Third Industrial Revolution" is misleading. It is not about a third epoch of industrialisation, but about the beginning of a de-industrialisation, the transition from the industrial to the information society.

Historic Separation?

In the 1960s and early 1970s, there was often talk of the Third World as the Third Sector of the world economy. Also then the Third World was not much more than an "imaginary community". But as such it had a certain significance in world politics. This implied not only its strategic role in the East-West conflict and its ideological function as the supporter of different "third paths" between capitalism and socialism. It was also about the Third World's attested "chaos power". That linked the fear (in the North) and the hope (in the South) that the developing countries would be in a position to cut off the industrial nations from supplies of important raw materials, thus putting them under pressure. But it was soon seen that both sides had over estimated this possibility, even with regard to oil. Instead of supply bottlenecks arising, raw materials prices plummeted. For some commodities, the fall in prices exceeded those of the Great Depression of 1929/30.

This was due, inter alia, to the conjunction of lower demand from the industrial nations and expansion of production by the raw material suppliers. Business activities dependent upon the supply of raw materials are tending to lose importance compared with the overall development of the global economy. The reason for this is to be seen in the transition from a material to an information economy.

This transition is taking place in line with the revolutionising of data transmission and the expansion of financial transactions which are not directly related to changes in the production of materials. The speed of the changes is remarkable.

However, the dematerialisation of business activities does not lead to decoupling of the Third World from the world economy. Declining market shares in world trade are not the expression of separation, but a loss of the affected countries positions in the world economy. Thus, the impact of dematerialisation is "only" that the negotiating positions of raw materials suppliers vis–a–vis the industrial nations will deteriorate further.

Differentiation of the Third World

But the radical change in the global economy is affecting some developing countries worse than others. Sub–saharan Africa and some countries in West and South Asia and Latin America are being pushed back further. The oil–producing countries with their high per capita export earnings will be able to hold their positions in the world economy for some time to come. The threshold countries of East and South-East Asia can expand theirs so long as they can continue to attract a growing share of global industrial production, and at the same time participate in the tertialisation of the world economy in the shape of rapidly-growing financial transactions. Thereby it should be noted that the degree of tertialisation in itself is not an adequate indicator for economic avant-gardism. Brazil exhibits a high degree of tertialisation in combination with a low macro-economic development dynamics. A good part of its tertialisation is being achieved by speculative financial transactions with their inherently greater risks and uncertainties than in the industrial countries. Such dangers have been demonstrated by Mexico's peso crisis and its repercussions on the whole of Latin America.

In some Third World countries, a "location annuity" has replaced the old raw materials one. Here it's about providing locations for off-shore transactions which offer international capital traders a maximum of freedom of movement combined with low taxation. Suitable for such operations are small countries which, despite low levy rates, achieve significant income in macro-economic terms.

The radical changes in the world economy are spurring the differentiation of the Third World without, however, necessarily fostering a dissolution of the Third World as an "imaginary community". It is precisely the advanced countries of East and South-East Asia that are showing a certain interest in the formulation of joint positions of the "South" in order to secure their own positional gains in the global economy. It's not by chance that the non-aligned countries and the Group of 77 have formed a joint coordination committee, and that the ASEAN countries are changing course on the international human rights policy.

Hitherto, the developing countries' strategy was to broaden the concept of human rights as a justification for demands on the industrial nations. But of late some developing countries, led by the ASEAN states, have questioned the universal validity of human rights even after their universality was confirmed by consensus at the Conference on Human Rights in Vienna in 1993. Playing a role in this policy is the governments' fear that due to the expansion of global communications networks, the behaviour patterns and preferences of their own people could in some way become similar to those of the West. As the rulers see it, that would be detrimental to the continuation of the development models practised so far.

Internet Creates New Cultural Dimension

Much information which Asian governments view as subversive in already globally available on the internet. The old struggle over the world information order, which at first was primarily a clinch between East and West, is thus taking on a new dimension. For with the growing importance of computer literacy to a country's ability to assert itself on world markets, the Asian threshold countries have not only an interest in controlling the on-line communication but also to expand it and the know-how that it requires.

Even the critics of any interventions in the internet and other global communications networks must admit that modern communication technologies are politically blind and their use in itself does not represent progress. The setting up and expansion of global information highways will offer forum not only to people who want to use it for education and enlightenment, but also to all shades of fundamentalists. These highways will not necessarily bring the misery of many Third World regions closer to the industrial countries, but possibly rather strengthen the tendency to process all world events as entertainment.

Global Two-thirds Society

The gravest aspect of the current upheaval in the world economy is its negative impact on jobs. The information economy needs for fewer workers than an economy based on materials. Instead, the demands on the skills of the workers are growing. Twenty per cent of the world workforce will in future be employed as (overworked) "intelligence workers". Eighty per cent will work part–time, if they are not underemployed or jobless. So the tertialisation of the global economy delivers more underemployment rather than more leisure time. The workers who are rationalised out of their jobs in the industrial sector cannot be absorbed by the service sector because it, too, is not left untouched by rationalisation measures. The civil service is also cutting back on staff. At all levels, there's a race to make the greatest possible savings on payrolls. At the same time, there's growing pressure to cut costs in providing for the victims of this development. That means thinning out the social security safety net.

The bottom line is that the two-thirds society, which developmental action groups hitherto assumed was limited to the Third World, is spreading worldwide. That, however, will not in the foreseeable future lead to an amendment of the North-South disparities. It's true that the change in the global economy is taking place faster, and to a greater extent in the industrial nations. But rationalisation is also happening in the developing countries in a bid to boost their competitiveness. So the upheaval in the world economy aggravates the problems which exist in a majority of the developing countries, while creating new ones in the

industrial nations. The need for action on the North-South
policy is growing, among the industrial nations. The need
for action on the North-South Policy is growing, while the
industrial nations' scope for concessions and compromises is
shrinking. The new social question which is now crystallising
at global level is not being answered. The consequences are
unforeseeable.

Another Loser?

It's more probable that a sharpening of the North–South
confrontation is to be reckoned with. For the industrial
nations will attempt to keep the social costs of the information
economy at bay for as long as possible. The trade unions
will thereby compete with the developing countries for jobs
for their members. But this policy has its limits precisely
because of the peaking of the problems in the industrial
nations. Overstepping these limits means war, and passively
accepting them chaos and social decay. Solutions could be
sought in two directions: effective taxation of the information
economies and the creation of jobs in the non-profit sector.
But it's possible there are no global solutions for global
problems. That would mean for at least part of the Third
World a renewal of the old debate on partial decoupling from
the world economy.

16

Crisis and New Orientation of Development Policy

The poverty in the South, the dislocations in the East, and the orientation crisis in the North are not isolated phenomena. Rather, they represent an alarming amalgamation of dangers that are globally interlinked.

The low effectiveness of international economic and development policy is rooted in two outdated paradigms on which the present worldwide strategy of economic development is based, namely that:

1. The Western social and economic model optimises the activation of productive forces—independent of the development stage of a country and its culture and therefore is best suited to satisfy basic needs;

2. It is possible to launch the development of a society from the outside within a few decades—without regard to is cultural and historical background—through external input of money, goods, technology, expertise, and personnel.

The twin paradigms of the timelessness and transferability combined with cultural ecological, and financial restrictions—have led international cooperation and development down the wrong path.

Only if we acknowledge the true dimensions of the global dangers, if we recognise the limitations and shortcomings of existing political instruments, and identify outdated theories and contradictory special interests, can we outline the cornerstones of a new policy of global cooperation.

Cornerstones of a New Development Policy

Starting with critical review of the shortcomings and paradigms of the prevailing development strategy, the following ten cornerstones of a new development policy are offered for discussion:

1. *Broaden the Concept of Development*

Whether a society is considered developed depends on the size of its per capita Gross National Product (GNP). Accordingly, the world is divided into a developed, semi developed, and underdeveloped world. The yardstick for development, which has become the norm in the industrial countries, is one-dimensional: It only measures the monetary value of goods and services that are exchanged in the marketplace. This standard is too narrow economically because it compresses the multitude and complexity of cultural, societal, historical. social,. and human values into a single economic category.

At the most, there can and should be agreement on what development and progress should not bring about: Inability to find enough work to meet the most basic needs; exploitation and oppression of people; loss of cultural wealth and institutions; destruction of natural resources. These, however, are the very values that are sacrificed by the prevailing development strategy. In the future, development policy must do all it can to stop the loss of skills and self-reliance, the plunder of natural resources, the erosion of cultural values, the violation of human dignity and human rights. Initiatives must prevail which are orientated on these values, and not just on the GNP.

2. *Concentrate Development Strategy on the Internal Potential of Developing Countries*

There must be an end to the manic fixation of development strategy on external inputs and external markets. A new development policy must, above all, improve internal conditions for a productive economy, promote domestic production factors on a broad basis, protect cultural and natural resources, and greatly increase the domestic supply of basic goods. Wherever external inputs are unavoidable, credits must be strictly tied to the productivity and the ability of a country to absorb transfers. External transfers should be concentrated on "Software" for health, education, social participation administative, and legal jurisdiction. Such an approach could also promote training and indigenous technologies, which are so important for economic development.

The set-up and expansion of the productive sectors must be decided, planned, and implemented by the developing countries themselves, and they must assume full responsibility. The external pressures, which force the developing countries into full integration with the world market, must be removed. This presupposes a structural reduction of interest rates.

3. Make Development Policy a Central Feature of Politics

Development policy must take the lead in mobilising the various political forces and government departments to join the fight against the growing global dangers. It must ensure that the actions of all political departments are compatible with development policy is possible only if it becomes the central task of all political sectors, comparable to social and environmental policies, and the central goal of all policies. If development policy is to become a central task, development problems must become a priority in parliament and government. Society must understand that it is in the national interest to accept great global responsibilities.

4. Reform the World Economy

The industrial countries must abolish their protectionism in agriculture 'as well the processed goods sector. Simultaneously, the developing countries need to be protected selectively and for a limited time against imports from the industrial countries. The undifferentiated structural adjustment policies imposed by the IMF must be revised. The trend toward regionalisation of the world economy should not be opposed; rather, in the interest of both South and East, it must be regulated constructively to form a new, regionally based world trade structure.

A reform of the international finance system is urgently needed: Interest and exchange rates should not "mirror the national interests of the big industrial states and the special interests of large banks and venture capital. Rather, they must reflect the global interest in monetary stability lower and stable interest rates, and sufficient development financing.

However, strengthening the international financial institutions is in the global interest only if the countries of the southern and eastern hemispheres are allowed to exert some influence. An international financial court must guarantee that violations of strict regulations to ensure international stability and solvency can be protested in a court of law.

5.   *Redesign the Industrial Society*

As a global social and environmental policy, the new development policy must induce the industrial countries to give up their excessive consumption of air, water, soil, resources, and space. Increased utilisation of energy-conservation measures and environmentally friendly technologies is overdue. The economic and social policies of the industrial nations must promote balance rather than growth. This requires radical changes in traditional economic thinking, habits, structures and processes.

In view of limited world resources, unsatisfied existential needs in South and East, and continuous population growth in the South, the only premise for the future can be: Growth rates in the South must be higher than in the North, but they should no longer be in the North, but they should no longer be induced primarily by growth in the North. If economic policies continue to call for the North to provide the locomotive, the North will have to continue to acquire more resources than the South.

The North must relinquish 'the remaining growth frontiers to the South and East. The South must use this opportunity to activate its internal dynamic potential rather than integrate its economy with the North. However, ecological and social controls must be established at a much earlier stage than was the case in Europe.

6. *Strengthen Development Cooperation*

The share of official development assistance as a percentage of GNP, which dropped from 0.48 per cent in 1982 to 0.34 per cent in 1995 must be gradually raised again and reach at least 0.7 per cent in the year 2000—a goal which OECD established as early as two decades ago and which was reconfirmed at the Rio Earth Summit.

However, we must not succumb to the illusion that a doubling of ODA funds will even remotely meet the financial needs of South and East. State development policy must use its scarce public funds more effectively in the future. It must use restraint whenever partners in the developing countries can accomplish a task on their own and private initiatives and private enterprise are more competent to do the job. The government should be directly engaged only when it can be relatively more productive. Otherwise, it should limit itself to subsidising private organisations.

7. *New Orientation for Development Cooperation*

The state and its implementation agencies must abandon all direct responsibility for any projects which require unbureaucratic action, economic efficiency, and long term productivity. It must make a much greater effort to involve NGO's and private venture capital in development projects. At the same time, the state must insist and guarantee that private actions are compatible with social and ecological concerns.

In the future, the main thrust of government projects should be the promotion of the internal potential of a country.

This comprises the political and administrative framework conditions of a humane, socially and ecologically sound development: Constitutional government, social institutions which facilitate broad participation of the population in politics, society, and economy; efficient savings, credit, fiscal and financial systems; mechanisms for income, property, and land distribution which promote productivity, justice, and social peace. In addition of this "software" of development, the following is needed: A regimen for the protection of resources and environment; measures to prevent the short term sellout of natural resources; elementary and general education and training, health care and social safety nets; capacities to develop science and technology.

8.   *Reduce the Debt Service and Activate Private Capital*

Public funds must be used to a greater degree for the financial rehabilitation of highly indebted countries in South and East; external demands for interest and principal payments must be adapted to the economic capacity of the respective country and its ability to execute external capital transfers.

Within the framework of international insolvency regulations, initiatives must be developed as a condition for the continuance of the present rules for write-offs—which ensure effective cooperation from the banks and alleviate the heavy burden of private credits, with their high interest rates.

State development policy and private business interests should supplement each other. Government promotion of private enterprise initiatives for exports, investment, and employment in the developing countries must take into account their compatibility with development. In reverse, private engagements which effectively promote development must be actively supported by the government. A separate line item must be established in the development budget for such activation of private capital.

9.   *Set Regional Priorities*

State development cooperation has been scattering its scarce funds not only among too many sectors, but also among too many partners. In the future, public funds must be concentrated regionally. More emphasis must be placed on regional programmes, and development cooperation with threshold countries must be enhanced. A portion of public funds should be set aside to provide an incentive for be set aside to provide an incentive for threshold countries to assist the poorer nations in their own region as well as deal with poverty in their own country.

The new development policy could then also help lessen ethnic-national conflicts and promote peace by sponsoring regional cooperation in joint development projects. For this purpose, regional development funds must be set up for cooperation in the transportation, energy, trade, and finance sectors and last, but not least for regional security systems and disarmament. Such regional funds could also provide the means to project refugees and improve their prospects for an eventual return to their homelands.

17

Population Growth and Education

In contrast to the food supply challenge posed by the coming wave of population growth, the global need for teachers and classrooms will rise very slowly in the next half-century. In many countries, the school-age population is increasing much less rapidly than the overall national population. The trend illustrates that growth rates typically differ for different age strata of the population. It has also shows that declining birth rates can take decades to move through an entire population.

At the global level, for example, total population is projected to increase by 54 per cent between 2000 and 2050, but the number of children aged 5 to 14 will grow by only 6 per cent. And of the world's largest countries—accounting for 60 per cent of global population in 1995—will actually begin to see decreases in the number of children aged 5 to 14 by 2015; for several of these countries, the decline in this age group has already begun. These countries will need fewer classrooms and teachers to educate the youngest members of society (assuming they maintain current class size and student-teacher ratios).

Plenty of nations, however, still have increasing child-age populations. Where countries have not acted to stabilise population, the base of the national population pyramid continues to expand, and pressures on the educational system will be severe. In the world's 10 fastest-growing countries, for example, most of which are in Africa and the Middle East, the child-age population will increase in average 93 per cent over the next half-century. Africa as a whole will see its school-age population grow by 75 per cent through 2040.

The rapid growth in African populations is especially worrisome because of the extra burden it imposes in a region already lagging in education. Only 56 per cent of Africans south of the Sahara are literate, compared with 71 per cent for all developing countries. Few African countries have universal primary education, and secondary education reaches only 4-5 per cent of African children. Educating today's children is challenge enough; the addition of another three students for every four already there will require heroic investments in education. But the alternative is grim: without additional investments in education, today's average student-teacher ratio of 42 in Sub-Saharan Africa will reach 75 by 2040.

Many countries will be challenged to increase funding for education while ensuring that other worthy sectors also receive the support they need. With 900 million illiterate adults in the world, the case for a renewed commitment to education is easy to make. But competing for these funds are the 840 million chronically hungry and the 1.2 billion without access to a decent toilet.

The budget stresses on governments attempting to meet these basic needs would clearly be reduced with smaller populations. Mozambique and Lesotho, for example, both met the UNESCO benchmark for investment in education in 1992; 6 per cent of gross domestic product—and the two countries economies were roughly equal in size. Yet because Mozambique has many times the population of Lesotho, spending per child in Lesotho is about nine times higher than in Mozambique. For the majority of countries who do not meet the UNESCO funding standard, many of whom also fall short in providing other basic services, a decline in population pressure could help substantially to meet all of their social goals.

If national education systems begin to stress life-long learning for a rapidly changing world, as recommended by a 1998 UNESCO report on education in the twenty-first century, then extensive provision for adult education will be necessary, affecting even those countries with shrinking childage populations. Such a development means that countries that started population stabilisation programmes earliest will be in the best position to educate their entire citizenry.

Pro-poor Tourism
Opportunities for Sustainable Local Development

Tourism is the world's largest industry, with over 10 per cent of GDP globally directly related to tourism activities. Rising standards of living in the countries of the North, declining long-haul travel costs, increasing holiday entitlements, changing demographics and strong consumer demand for exotic international travel have resulted in significant tourism growth to developing countries. Tourism is the principal export for one-third of developing countries. Tourism brings relatively powerful consumers to Southern countries, potentially an important market for local entrepreneurs and an engine for local sustainable economic development. There is no reliable data on domestic tourism but it is growing rapidly in South America and in China and South East Asia; it represents a very significant economic opportunity for many local communities.

Tourism and Aid

Multilateral and bilateral aid agencies are wary of involving themselves in the tourism sector. In 1969 the World Bank created a Tourism Projects Department recognising that in the Mediterranean and Adriatic countries, and in Mexico, tourism had been a significant generator of foreign exchange and of direct and indirect employment, internationally in the late nineteen sixties, there was considerable concern about high rates of unemployment and the ability of developing countries to service debt. Tourism sector studies were completed in some 31 countries and tourism staff regularly participated in World Bank macroeconomic missions—their reports focussed on the potential for growth in tax revenues, foreign exchange earnings and direct and indirect employment effects. The primary emphasis was on national economic impact. By 1978 when the World Bank closed its Tourism Projects Department of the Bank had provided loans and credits for 18 projects in 14 countries and it was the major source of funds and technical assistance for tourism development. The bank withdrew from tourism development for a range of reasons amongst which were anxieties about the role of the bank in funding projects to develop luxury hotels designed to attract wealthy travellers from the developed countries. This strategy was seen inconsistent with new policy objectives which prioritised the bottom 40 per cent, the Bank's priorities were shifting towards the poor, a group, which was gaining relatively little from tourism development. There was a growing literature that focussed on the negative economic, social and cultural impacts of unmanaged tourism on local communities. The fuel crises of the nineteen seventies also undermined some of the forecasts that had been made for the strength of the market and the Bank withdrew from the sector in parallel with most other multilateral and bilateral agencies.

The international agencies followed a macro-economic tourism agenda in the nineteen seventies and eighties focussing on tax and foreign exchange revenues at the national level, major hotel and resort development, international promotion and national and regional master planning all attracted funding. In the nineties the adoption of the new poverty elimination target of halving the number of people living on less than 1 US $ per day by 2015 refocussed development assistance on pro-poor growth. Multilateral and bilateral aid agency agendas are shifting towards micro economic strategies, which benefit local communities and in particular those below the poverty threshold. With poverty elimination now at the heart of decision aid, the potential for using tourism to generate pro-poor economic growth is being reassessed.

Since the mid-1980s, interest in 'green' tourism, eco-tourism and community tourism has grown rapidly among tour operators, policy makers, advocates and researchers. All of these focus on the need to ensure that tourism does not erode the environmental and cultural base on which it depends. The emphasis has been on minimising social, cultural and environmental impacts; rather than on positively affecting the livelihoods of the poor.

The Potential of Pro-poor Tourism

There are a number of reasons to look again at tourism and to assess its potential to generate pro-poor growth, 80 per cent of the world's poor live in just 12 countries and tourism is significant or growing in all but one of them. Tourism is a very large sector, it is growing rapidly, and there is some evidence that it is relatively labour intensive. The consumer travels to the destination, creating additional—local—opportunities for the sale of additional goods and services—ranging from local pottery to a guided walk. Tourism can be used to diversify local economies; it can often be developed in remote and marginal areas with few other diversifications or export opportunities. These areas often attract tourists because of their high landscape, cultural and wildlife values. These natural resources and the local culture are amongst the few assets of the poor.

Pro-poor tourism generates net benefits for the poor. It can be defined as forms of tourism where the benefits to the poor are greater than costs which tourism brings them. Economic costs and benefits are clearly important but social environmental and cultural costs and benefits are clearly important, but social and benefits also need to be taken into account. Pro-poor tourism aims to expand opportunities for those living on less than 1 US$ per day. Whilst it will also need to be sustainable preserving local culture, minimizing environmental impacts, it will be driven by the poverty agenda. Community-based tourism seeks to promote initiatives by local communities or individuals within them; much has been learnt from these projects. Maximising the poverty elimination effect requires that the emphasis is placed on involving those people who are living on less than 1 US$ per day and creating economic opportunities for them. Not all community tourism is pro-poor in this sense.

Effects on the Livelihoods of the Poor

Assessing the livelihood impacts of tourism is not simply a matter of counting jobs or wage income. Participatory poverty assessments demonstrate great variety in the priorities of the poor and factors affecting livelihood security and sustainability. Tourism can affect many of these, positively and negatively, often indirectly. It is important to assess these impacts and their distribution.

Tourism can generate four different types of local cash income generally involving different categories of people:

* wages from formal employment;

* earnings from selling goods, services, or casual labour (e.g., food, crafts, building materials, guide services);

* and profits arising from locally owned enterprises;

* Income: this may include profits from a community run enterprise, dividends from a private sector partnership and land rental paid by an investor.

Waged employment can be sufficient to lift a household from insecure to secure. But it may only be an available to a minority, and not to the poor. Casual earnings per person may be very small, but much more widely spread and may be enough, for instance, to cover school fees for one or more children. Work as a tourist guide although casual, is often of high status and relatively well paid. There are relatively few examples of successful and sustainable collective income from tourism.

Negative economic impacts include inflation, dominance by outsiders in land markets and in-migration, which erodes economic opportunities for the local poor. Impacts differ between men and women. Women can be the first to suffer from loss of natural resources (e.g., access to fuel wood) and cultural/sexual exploitation, but may benefit most from physical infrastructure improvements (e.g. piped water or a grinding mill) where this is a by-product of tourism.

Positive Development Impacts of Tourism

On the positive side, tourism can generate funds for investments in health, education and other assets, provide infrastructure, stimulate development of social capital, strengthen sustainable management of natural resources, and create a demand for improved assets (especially education). On the negative side, tourism can reduce local access to natural resources draw heavily upon local infrastructure, and disrupt social networks.

Tourism affects the livelihoods of the poor by changing their access to assets. In several cases, tourism's impact on people's access to natural resources or physical infrastructure has been identified as the most important benefit or concern.

Cultural Impacts of Tourism Can be Positive or Negative

Local residents often highlight the way tourism affects other livelihood goals—whether positively or negatively—such as cultural pride, a sense of control, good health, and reduced vulnerability. Socio-cultural intrusion by tourists is often cited as a negative impact. Certainly sexual exploitation particularly affects the poorest women, girls and young men. The poor themselves may view other types of cultural change as positive. Tourism can also increase the value attributed to minority cultures by national policy-makers. Overall, the cultural impacts of tourism are hard to disentangle from wider processes of development.

The overall balance of positive and negative livelihood impacts will vary enormously between situations, among people and over time, and particularly in the extent to which local priorities are able to influence the planning process.

The application of a 'sustainable' livelihood framework is essential to developing pro-poor approaches. The distribution of livelihood impacts has to be considered. The poor are far from being a homogenous group. The positive and negative impacts of tourism will inevitably be distributed unevenly among poor groups, reflecting different patterns of assets, activities, opportunities and choices. The most substantial benefits, particularly jobs, may be concentrated among few. Net benefits are likely to be smallest, or negative, for the poorest.

Policies to Enhance Pro-Poor Tourism

Despite innumerable case studies of tourism development, there is relatively little assessment of practical experience in strategies to make tourism more pro-poor. Nevertheless, lessons can be drawn from a wealth of small initiatives (many from 'community tourism' or 'conservation and development' programmes), supplemented by expanding knowledge on 'pro-poor growth strategies', several policy implications clearly emerge.

1. *Put Poverty Issues on the Tourism Agenda*

A first step is to recognise that enhancing the poverty impacts of tourism is different from commercial, environmental or ethical concerns. PPT can be incorporated as an additional objective, but this requires pro-active and strategic intervention. There may well be trade-offs to make- for example between attracting all-inclusive operators and maximising informal sector opportunities, or between faster growth through outside investment, and slower growth building on local capacity. These trade-offs need to be addressed.

2. *Enhance Economic Opportunities and a Wide Range of Impacts*

Two approaches need to be combined:

•   Expand poor people's economic participation by addressing the barriers they face, and maximising a wide range of employment, self-employment and informal sector opportunities;

* Incorporate wider concerns of the poor into decision-making. Reducing competition for natural resources, minimising trade-offs with other livelihood activities, using tourism to create physical infrastructure that benefits the poor and addressing cultural disruption will often be particularly important.

3. *A Multi-level Approach*

Pro-poor interventions can and should be taken at three different levels:

* this is where pro-active practical partnerships can be developed between operators, residents, NGOs and local authorities, to maximise benefits;

* national policy level—policy reform may be needed on a range of tourism issues (planning, licensing, training) and non-tourism issues (land tenure, business incentives, infrastructure, land-use planning);

* International level—to encourage responsible consumer and business behaviour, and to enhance commercial codes of conduct.

4. *Work through Partnerships, Including Business and Tourists*

National and local governments, private enterprises, industry associations, NGOs, community organisations, consumers, and donors all have a role to play. It is particularly important to engage business, and to ensure that initiatives are commercially realistic and integrated into main stream operations. Private operators will not be able to devote substantial time and resources to developing pro-poor actions. NGOs and donors can help in reducing the transaction costs of changing commercial practice—for example, facilitating the training, organisation, and communication that would enable businesses to use more local suppliers. Changing the attitudes of tourists (at both international and national levels) is also essential if pro-poor tourism is to be commercially viable and sustainable.

5. *Incorporate Pro-poor Tourism Approaches into Mainstream Tourism*

Pro-poor tourism should not just be pursued in niche markets (such as eco-tourism or community tourism). It is even more important that mass tourism is developed in ways that benefit the poor. It is also important to assess which tourism segments are particularly relevant to poor. Domestic tourists are likely to be important customers.

6. *Reform Decision-Making Systems*

It is impossible to prescribe exactly how each tourism enterprise should develop in ways that best fit with livelihoods. The most important principle is to enhance the participation of the poor. Three different ways of doing this can be identified:

- Strengthen rights at local level (e.g., tenure over tourism assets), so that local people have market power and make their own decisions over developments;

- Develop more participatory planning;

- Use planning gain and other incentives to encourage private investors to enhance local benefits. These approaches require implementation capacity among governmental and non-governmental institutions within the destination, and require a supportive national policy framework.

It is time to reconsider the role of tourism in contributing to pro-poor development. Tourism should be judged against other possible strategies and where it offers the best opportunities for pro-poor growth, or where it can make a useful contribution by increasing the diversity of opportunities for the poor, tourism it should be considered. However, careful and effective local management will be essential if it is to contribute to meeting poverty targets and if tourism dependency is to be avoided.

❊ ❊ ❊

19

Consumption Bomb

It is three decades since we passed the peak world population growth rate of 2.04 per cent. Annual additions too are now a decade past their peak of 86 million a year. They are currently running at 78 million a year and are heading downwards. A peak in total numbers, however, still lies at least four or five decades ahead. On the UN Population Division's 1998 projections, the total is likely to reach 8.9 billion in 2050. The long range medium projection, which has not been updated since 1996, expects world population to level out at just under 11 billion in 2200 AD.

However, this is based on assumptions that are increasingly questionable. More and more countries are reaching levels of female fertility that are not enough for replacement—below 2.1 children over the lifetime of each women. At the latest count there are 61 countries in this category. Of this 23 had very low fertility, below 1.5.

The situation is unprecedented in times of global peace on economic growth. The UN medium projection assumes that where fertility is very low it will rise again to 1.7-1.9 children per woman. In all countries where fertility is currently above replacement level of 2.1, it assumes that it will not fall below that level.

Yet fertility has fallen below replacement level in so many countries, which such different cultures and different stages of economic growth, that is increasingly looking as if low fertility may be here to stay. If this became the case, then world population may peak at somewhere between 8 and 9 billion. Thereafter it may well begin to decline. The 1996 long range low projection has world population falling to 5.6 billion in 2100 AD.

None of this means that reproductive rights should have lower priority in future. Their contribution to the health and welfare of women and children are clear. Many poor countries in Africa and South Asia face huge population increases which will be hard to accommodate without major problems of land and water scarcity. In these areas reproductive rights receive a very high priority.

Increasingly our concern must focus on consumption, and how we can cope with the effects of its inexorable increase. Over the past 25 years world population increased by 53 per cent, but world consumption per person (Measured by income) by only 39 per cent. Assume that consumption per person will rise 100 per cent, while population will rise by only half that amount. As time goes on the preponderance of consumption will increase more and more.

There is a crucial difference between population and consumption aspirations. If fully assured of children's survival most people have quite modest desire for family size. But their desire to consume knows no upper bounds. As wealth increases, people double-up their possessions; two or three cars, two bathrooms, two rooms with all contents, two or three holidays a year.

Appliances improve every year and old ones "need" replacing. New needs are created that never existed before. Globalisation is making products cheaper than ever. TVs are no longer uncommon even in African shanty towns. The number of households is increasing as people live longer and family breakdown becomes more common. Smaller households consume considerably more per per cent than large. Moreover, consumption is politically very difficult to restrain. No one can get elected promising people they can earn and spend less, or re-elected if they fulfil their promises.

In view of this much of the burden of reducing our environmental impact will rest on technology. Technology will have to deliver major shifts in improving resource productivity, and in reducing the amount of waste we create. All our institutions and forms of management which affect technology will need to be geared to this end.

In some areas the record has been good and looks likely to remain so. Productivity has kept up with demand in the case of resources that are traded on markets, and that are under the direct control of people or companies affected by shortages or prices. Global food production has kept pace with demand: although land and cereal production per person has declined, average intakes of calories and protein have continued to improve and are at record levels. Malnutrition persists, but this is due to poverty and landlessness, not to the inability of the world to produce enough food. We have not encountered any limiting shortage of any key mineral resources or of energy. Nor are we likely to, because we continually economise and find substitutes, there has been a gradual reduction in the material used for each unit of production.

The prospects are much worse for resources that are not traded on markets or subject to sustainable management, as yet. These include groundwater, state forests, ocean fish, biodiversity in general. They include communal waste sinks like rivers, lakes and oceans, and the global atmosphere. In all of these areas it looks likely that things will get quite a lot worse before they get better.

These kinds of resources and sinks are not under the direct control of people affected by shortage or damage. People wishing to change the way a common resource or sink is used or managed have to pass through the legal or political system. They must organise, take out lawsuits against polluters, pressurise legislators and so on. Political responses are typically slow. Usually the majority of voters have to be convinced of the need for action before politicians will risk taking action. Even then powerful and rich vested interest will lobby hard for the status quo, and will often succeed in frustrating changes that are desired by a global majority. America's coal, oil, and car lobbies have stood in the way of any significant US commitment to reduce carbon-di-oxide output, and the US is the world's largest emitter of carbon-di-oxide.

Usually there has to be very widespread and very visible environmental damage before action is taken. The thinning of the ozone layer fitted that category well and the response was swift. North Atlantic fishing reached that point in the 1990s, yet politicians shied away from taking adequate action until the last moment: fishing stocks plummeted and there was massive job loss. Global warming is still long way from the damage being widespread enough, and attributable clearly enough to human activities, for politicians to be ready to speed up the move into renewable energy.

The question with the common resources and sinks is always: will we react in time? The answer is all the more difficult because we usually don't know in advance what is "in time." Many critical changes are subject to threshold effects. When a certain point is crossed, very sudden and disastrous change can occur with little warning. In many cases we do not know where the thresholds lie.

Prudence dictates a preventive approach—a stitch in time saves nine. But the history of environmental problems shows that politicians rarely act decisively until the brink is reached, and it will always be touch and go whether we are pushed over it or not.

❋ ❋ ❋

20

The World Bank Needs Innovative Theory

The World Bank's macro-economic assumptions disregard many issues relevant to development. These include, for instance, population growth and income distribution. Endogenous growth models are better suited to analyse complex interactions than the conventional tools of neoclassic and post-Keynesian economics.

The World Bank is officially committed to sustainable development. Yet its own policy does not adhere to this principle. Structural adjustment programmes and poverty reduction strategies still conflict with social and ecological goals. One reason for the poor sustainability record is the World Bank's outdated theoretical approach based on neoclassic and post-Keynesian ideas.

Both are incompatible with sustainability. Neoclassic understanding of sustainability rests on the belief that technological progress automatically leads to a more efficient use of resources and, accordingly, to less ecological degradation.

For several reasons, post-Keynesian models are similarly incompatible with the principle of sustainability. First of all, they produce analyses for the short term. Typically, merely two periods are considered, which is inadequate for designing a growth process in general and even more so for a sustainable path to development. Moreover, these models also disregard distribution because they only take aggregated quantities into account.

World Bank economists, however, still work with country-specific variants of the post-Keynesian Revised Minimum Standard Model, although it is academically outdated and cannot deal with the complexity of development processes. The model's merits are that it is easy to understand and apply. In addition, little information on the behaviour of the economic actors is required. The World Bank determines the volume of its loans on the basis of such calculations. In addition to the transfer of these sums, the bank believes that measures to promote growth are necessary. These are expected to be in line with the Washington Consensus approach of privatisation, deregulation and liberalisation.

The structural and stabilisation measures that the World Bank economists implement are thus based on theoretical models which are incompatible with the principle of sustainability and which they, at most, supplement with cushioning elements. The obvious alternative would be to apply more recent approaches of endogenous growth theory. After all, economic growth is a precondition for sustainable development. Endogenous growth models are very diverse, so one cannot speak of an integrated and comprehensive theory. However, all endogenous models share the attempt to explain growth without recourse to exogenous factors. While the basic model of endogenous growth theory was developed for industrialised nations, it can be adapted to situations typical of developing countries. This gives an idea of the complex interrelatedness of economic phenomena.

Complex Interactions

These manifold links clearly serve to illustrate the shortcomings of the World Bank. For example, the IMF and the World Bank call for the immediate opening of national economies to world trade. By contrast, endogenous growth models suggest assessing free trade's benefits for developing countries more diligently. Trade liberalisation only presents an opportunity to increase long-term growth rates in developing countries when pursued in a differentiated way respecting specific needs of countries and sectors. Otherwise, there is a risk of economies specialising solely on low-technology goods, which, in turn, means forsaking long-term innovation.

Complementary measures are necessary if developing countries are to take advantage of liberalisation. Education, enhancement of communications and transport infrastructure and special mechanisms for the transfer of knowledge from advanced to developing countries (such as on-the-job-training, imitation of existing technologies and foreign direct investment) are important determinants for economic development. The level of education in a developing country is particularly significant. If a national economy has too little human capital, opening the markets mostly results in minor or even negative growth effects. Empirical studies support these statements.

Population growth is a serious obstacle to development. In may poor regions, it puts the already overburdened education and health systems under additional stress. Traditional economics theory, however, ignores the significance of fertility. Endogenous growth models can take family planning into account and link birth rates to social security systems as well as to environmental aspects. Doing so leads to developmental insights. For instance, short-term social cushioning measures, such as those implemented frequently by the World Bank and its partners to reduce the negative impacts of programme-tied loans, do not suffice for a positive development process. By contrast, long-term social security measures (such as introducing a pension scheme) contribute to reducing fertility.

Poverty Stalls Growth

Incomes in developing countries are mostly distributed very unevenly. The World Bank, so far, does not view this as an important obstacle to development. At any rate, the widespread thesis that, in the wake of economic development, inequality first increases and then decreases by itself has empirically been shown to be wrong. Endogenous growth models under pin this finding in theoretical terms. Unequal income distribution results in too little investment in training, the consequences of which impede growth.

Endogenous models are also useful from an ecological viewpoint. According to neoclassic environmental and resources theory, external effects of noxious emissions and over-exploitation of resources must be internalised in order to ensure long-term economic growth. Instruments in tune with the market, such as taxes or certificates, are better suited to do so than strict governmental regulation. Even these findings are not yet paid enough attention in the Country Assistance Strategies in which the World Bank lays down short-to medium-term development strategies.

Endogenous growth theory contributes to analysing the complex interactions of sustainable development. Even if most of the recommendations are well established in the critique of developmental practice, formal theoretical analyses help to avoid the arbitrariness of policy statements. Future research must show how to develop a user-friendly, comprehensive. Building on a profound analysis of development determinants, it will be possible to draft country specific development strategies in line with sustainability principles. These should be reflected in the conditionalities of programme-tied loans. To ensure consistent implementation of sustainable development policy, the World Bank must update its theoretical models. Endogenous growth theory provides a starting point.

21

Making the Multilateral System Work

International institutions are, as yet, too weak to ensure the provision of global public goods. It is not enough to merely defend the multilateral system against attacks. Its shortcomings must be acknowledged in order to find ways to a better future.

Nation states cannot establish security, prosperity and freedom on their own. In a globally networked world, constant policy failure looms unless there is cross-border cooperation. Yet instead of a multilateral drive to shape globalisation, we are witnessing a manifest crisis of multilateralism. This is not only a question of the Iraq war or of stagnation in the cases of the World Trade Organisation and the Kyoto Protocol. With good reason, critics of multilateralism point to the international system's bureaucratic Molochs, the rapid spread of institutions and the (frequently ineffective) proliferation of international conferences, decision and agendas. Moreover, elected politicians fear that the trend towards making decisions in systems of international negotiation will rob parliaments of their legitimate political power.

Talk of multilateralism's failure, however, might yet prove premature. The US government is now learning that, while it can win wars single-handedly, it, nevertheless, depends on alliances and the legitimatising authority of UN in order to establish peace, security and democracy. Perhaps, the shock of Cancun will soon lead to a willingness of the industrialised nations to compromise in the agricultural sector. A collapse of the world trade system would definitely not suit them.

Yet even if the pressure of global problems were to turn into a motor for multilateralism, that in itself would not iron out the weaknesses of the existing multilateral system. Shortcomings are becoming ever more apparent as the relevance of international coordination for national societies increases. Whoever believes that multilateralism is necessary must name its problems. As in the European Union, a lack of institutional reform is threatening to result in an incapacity to act.

It is not enough merely to defend the present institutions against the attacks of unilateralism. The prerequisites of a more effective multilateralism must yet be fulfilled. International coordination means designing policy in complex negotiating systems without the institutionally embedded hierarchies known in national government systems. This implies a host of problems—such as the great number of participants, decisions based on the lowest common denominator, the length of the negotiating processes and, not least, the manifold opportunities powerful actors have to evade international rules.

For international development cooperation, the efforts and debates concerning budget financing, programme assistance and coordinated sectoral projects by the donor community are similar relevance. The great crises of human kind cannot he mastered by single projects that are both costly and small-scale.

An agenda to strengthen multilateralism in development cooperation must go beyond these piecemeal approaches. Global policy needs a coherent structure of global governance. Therefore the agenda should include the following, certainly conflict-prone, questions:

• How can the effectiveness and efficiency of multilateral development organisations be strengthened'? Which organisations have operational capacities? Which organisations should focus on coordinating, moderating or initiating programmes and agenda-setting'?

- How can sector-oriented multilateral organisations (such as the WTO, the World Health Organisation and the United Nations Environment Programme) contribute to getting a grip on trans-sector problems (such as climate change, disintegrating societies and population growth)? How can contradictions within the multilateral system's fragmented rules be overcome?

- How is overlap-stemming from multiple jurisdictions and parallel agendas within the multilateral system—be avoided? How can the cooperation of organisations be improved on the basis of their respective specialisation advantages? Which organisations or special programmes have become redundant and should be discontinued?

- How can actors (not only governments) from developing countries become responsible and appropriately represented players in the international system—especially in the World Bank and the International Monetary Fund? The buzzwords of experts are voice, capacity-building and power-sharing. Reforms are necessary to increase the effectiveness and legitimation of the institutions. On the other hand, The actors in the industrialised nations must not withdraw from these institutions as that would degrade them to scarcely effective discussion forums as has happened, for instance, to the UN Conference on Trade and Development (UNCTAD).

- How can internationally agreed standards (such as, for instance, the central norms of the International Labour Organisation) actually be enforced? Otherwise multilateral institutions will remain toothless. What options are there for imposing sanctions? So far, due to the modus operandi of international law, powerful countries that flout international rules have been less hampered in their actions than actors who violate rules in the context of constitutionally regulated states. International agreements often lack mechanisms to punish rule infringements.

- What minimum standards should apply in future with respect to accountability, transparency and participation by societal actors? Anti-globalisation movements, civil societies accustomed to democracy, and parliaments claim the right to participate and cannot be simply disregarded.

The list of the challenges could easily go on. We are, indeed, dealing with Herculean tasks. For day-to-day politics, this is not a field that promises the quick score of "merit points", But whoever is concerned with the future of global society will have to come to grips with the difficult fundamentals and preconditions of a more effective multilateralism. Europe's national governments and the European Commission must ask themselves whether they have appropriate strategies for the future of multilateral organisations and whether they provide them with adequate resources.

Most likely, pioneer groups and progressive "coalitions of the willing" (frequently also called "Iikeminded states") will more and more often lead the way by seeking solutions to world problems even if other countries do not follow suit. It is about linking governments with other actors that want to forge ahead quickly in this field.

❋ ❋ ❋

Aid Effectiveness as a Multi-Level Process

Parallel to the widespread decrease of aid resources provided by donor countries to developing countries in recent years, debate and research on how to make aid more effective has become a major concern. Usually, it is suggested that decades of development assistance have at best produced marginal results in terms of improving development levels in the South. Little mention is made of donor's policy shortcomings and the negative impact of these on efforts aimed at reforming and redefining development cooperation in order to enhance aid effectiveness. The policy parameters and operating frameworks of existing and policies continue to inhibit higher degree of aid effectiveness. In many donor countries, opinion polls indicate waning public support for development aid.

Increasingly, the moral case for aid is called into question and deeper world market integration tends to be seen as the panacea to continued economic decline and social destabilisation in the South. Against this background, cooperation between donor and recipient actors is faced with a duel uphill struggle. First, fewer resources can be mobilised to meet growing developmental needs. On the other hand, to organise and manage development policies and programmes in result-oriented manner, grows more difficult. The threat of further aid cuts and of further drops of public support for providing aid become ever more real. A closer look at the organisational complexities and political constraints under which development cooperation is expected to perform effectively may help to improve current aid management approaches.

Towards Conceptual Clarity

At first sight, catchy definitions of what constitutes effective aid might appear attractive to use, in particular with regard to economic indicators. The term "aid effectiveness" is easily used in the same vein as "efficiency", "significance" or "impact" of aid. At times, obsession to measure and demonstrate the results of aid supported development processes can be observed among policy-makers and administrators on the donor side. Still the understanding of aid and its effectiveness as being part and parcel of a cooperation relationship between donor and recipient side parties, is scarcely embedded in practice. To determine how to make aid more effective requires more than a quick impact analysis of an individual and perhaps even isolated development project. Consequently, defining the concept of aid effectiveness needs to take into account at what levels cooperation is focused on. To strive for sustainable and effective modes of development cooperation will entail the need to combine recipient ownership of the development process with donor accountability concerns.

Performance expectations cannot be exclusively placed on the recipient while donor interests, their aid management systems and procedures remain unchanged.

An extended and more analytical, process oriented definition should take into account four main aspects of aid effectiveness:

(a) Effective aid must relate to the building and/or strengthening of in-country aid management capacity;

(b) To maximise the degree of aid effectiveness, local ownership of the aid process is essential: from setting of priorities through policy formulation and implementation on to the evaluation stages of the process;

(c)   Increasing recipient side capabilities to take charge of aid relationship, will need to be combined with arrangements to meet legitimate donor accountability concerns;

(d)   Aid effectiveness is a two-faceted objective: its realisation is equally dependent on increased transparency of donor motives and on dropping of non-developmental, political and economic aid objectiveness of donors.

In addition a broader range of stakeholders in the aid relationship needs to be actively involved: extending beyond accountable government and implementing agencies, to include democratic institutions and organisations of civil society and of the private sector.

Applying any definition of aid effectiveness without disaggregating macro-economic data and taking into account country specificity will only lead to unhelpful generalisations about aid and its effectiveness. It would seem more appropriate to adopt working definitions against which to assess effectiveness of aid resources at a country-specific level. On such a basis one could expect to arrive at more reliable indicators of how well aid resources contribute to improving developmental standards and meeting existing needs.

From Definition to Success—Key Requirements

Having reached agreement between the recipient and donor on what should constitute effectiveness of aid is only a starting point. Embarking on democratic, peaceful and participatory patterns of economic and social development must follow: to arrive at significant and lasting improvements in many of the least developed countries will be a long-term process. This being said, it is crucial to design and implement such forms of development cooperation which involve a wide range of recipient side actors, not only from the government side but also from civil society at large. Seen as a process of increasing inclusion of intended beneficiaries of aid, the commitment to decentralise as well as entrust aid and its management grows in importance.

` To fully capture Third World development realities, policy frameworks inspired by neoliberalist-type of development concepts and theories are grossly inadequate. The views and positions on aid articulated in the World Bank and the IMF, or in many if not most bilateral aid administrations in OECD countries, represent only one side of today's international cooperation, namely the donor side. The major weakness to point out with respect to this locus of debate, is a profound under-representation if not even a total absence of recipient experiences and perceptions on aid in general and on its effectiveness in particular. There should be little doubt that ignoring or not actively identifying and involving such perceptions, leads to strongly donor driven aid.

To circumvent recipient side insights and views on strengths and weaknesses of aid strategies and mechanisms, will result in limited local commitment and sense of ownership over the aid process. Mutual decision-making between donors and recipients remains a rare policy approach. Aid procedures that are based on local management and less control-oriented donor roles in the aid process are still exceptions in development cooperation.

Structurally, in terms of the policy environment within which development aid is expected to function, the overriding policy framework is general based on structural adjustment policies (SAP). But the underlying conclusion made by proponents of SAPs that these policies induce aid effectiveness, has yet to be proven valid. It must suffice at this point to emphasize that there is not a priori relationship between world market integration under structural adjustment and sustainable development in poor countries. Aid to these countries which is solely intended to reinforce fundamentally uneven and unequal patterns of world market integration should at be scrutinised critically.

Some central issues need to be addressed in the course of improving aid and its effectiveness:

- institutional dimensions of aid relationships require strong policy-attention, both on the donor and the recipient side;

- capacities to effectively identify and formulate aid priorities need to be strengthened in recipient countries;

- local capacities to sustain reform efforts must be reinforced.

Levels of Intervention

If the design of aid and the terms upon which it is provided to a developing country are largely determined by the donor, the aid relationship can be characterised as essentially hierarchical. Recipient side views will rarely surface, as they are either not identified, or not well formulated. Possibilities of a recipient-led development strategies can be limited. Unless scope is provided to the recipient side actors to assume responsibilities, aid effectiveness is likely to remain low or fluctuating, and the sustainability of donor aid efforts will remain doubtful.

National planning processes and courses of national development in recipient countries should be seen as most effective where they are led under local responsibility and control. To arrive at this ideal situation, gaps need to be reduced and closed at the various intervention levels.

Donor aid resources provide valuable support for this process. Their effectiveness in meeting long-term objective of aid will need to be assessed on the basis of how well they perform at the different levels. Individual donors will expectedly perform differently at the various levels. What will prove to be the ultimate test for effectiveness is how well the donor aid performance accomplishes the broader objectives of development cooperation and how well it includes sustainable results.

In the analytical framework outlined here, development cooperation would seem to be confronted with the effectiveness gaps at the:

- *Structural level:* International trade and investment patterns, debt problems and world market integration process appear as long-term constraining factors upon aid and its effectiveness;

- *At the policy level,* dialogue and partnership in development cooperation are instrumental factors in recluding planning and co-ordination gaps with regard to policy analysis and formulation;

- *The institutional level* is where pertinent capacity gaps exist: capacity development efforts of donors and technical assistance measures play an important role in addressing weaknesses in aid effectiveness within a country's institutional setting;

- Finally, at the *level of aid projects* (programmes), it is generally the lack of sustainability of aid interventions which causes development activities to falter once donor support decreases or stops. In addition to technical cooperation, financial and material inputs serve to maintain project momentum and goal realisation: the issue of how to develop local capacity sufficiently in order for indigenous organisations to continue project activities initially supported by donor aid, remains the most important issue to address at this level.

Fostering Aid Effectiveness

Donor and recipient development efforts are too often isolated from one another, or poorly coordinated. They fail to address managerial and implementation bottlenecks. Cross-sectorial linkages, as well as inter-disciplinary approaches to aid problems are only slowly gaining ground. It is increasingly obvious that decisions on aid issues are subjected to concerns outside to the responsible ministry: finance ministers, economics ministers and unfortunately even defense ministers have a strong say in how much aid is to be provided, where it is to be concentrated and under what terms to be utilised. Inside of recipient countries, large portions of national budgets are allocated to non-development priorities with little or no impact on alleviating urgent poverty problems.

Development cooperation may make the biggest impact and be executed most effectively where donors and recipients agree upon multi-level aid strategies. To give an example: building a road to a remote rural area may well be done in an effective project manner: it is equally important to have a functioning transport authority in place to ensure maintenance of the roads. If this authority operates within a nationally defined infrastructure policy, best in accord with national trade and investment priorities, then the effectiveness of the project-level road building programme has a good chance of being high.

Institutional changes to set the stage for a profound reform process in development cooperation are needed. Reprioritising national budgets to reflect identified in-country development needs may be one step. Setting up policy evaluation and formulation units can be complimentary measures. Deregulating markets and investment rules may serve to please donors, but dumping of cheap products which strangle local production efforts may easily result. Regional cooperation, including intensified South-South cooperation can provide some counterbalance. There are only a few areas where changes in the current system of development cooperation can occur, with a view to better manage the complexities of aid and the social, cultural, economic and political backgrounds against which they take place. The will and commitment to take policy action in both donor and recipient countries, through the broadest range of stakeholders and institutions as possible, will be the test for genuine efforts at improving development relations between North and South and organising cooperation effectively.

❉ ❉ ❉

Democracy and the Market Economy

Today the idea of democracy is triumphant; the model is in principle embraced in most countries the world over. You may say that the very word democracy has been hailed and misused earlier in history. The most repressing and totalitarian regimes have tried to mask themselves as "real" or "peoples" democracies. What has happened, however, is a historical demasking of these false pretences.

What exactly do we mean by democracy? There is now a general agreement that democracy cannot be defined by purpose or policy or levels of mass mobilisation. It must be defined as a political system where different parties or individuals compete for power through regular free elections where all adult citizens have a vote. Moreover, a democracy must uphold certain basic human rights and well-defined freedoms which make the political process possible, and respect the opinion and integrity of the individual. No other definitions hold, and we should be careful when we talk about "real" democracy versus "formal" democracy. A society which in real life upholds the constitutional or formal democratic principles and which in practice applies the rights these principles imply, is by definition a democracy. A society with a beautiful sounding constitution but where none or few of these rights are respected is certainly not a democracy.

Democratic Government no Guarantee for Equality

It is important to understand that democratic government, does not necessarily mean good government in the sense that those in power make wise or well-considered decisions. Nor does it mean that conflicts inherent in the society are reduced to a minimum. Demands for democracy, social justice and a better life have historically gone hand in hand, but this does not mean that the establishment of a democratic system actually does lead to an improvement in social conditions or equality. It is also quite clear that some societies have a sort of outer shell of democracy but in reality, exclude large groups of people from having any political influence whatsoever. The actual differences in living conditions are so enormous and so entrenched that these people have no confidence at all in the political system even if it is democratic according to the definition. In these cases, for example in some Latin American countries, one can talk of a "masked hegemony with competing elites" where the outcome of struggles for power has little relevance for the masses. It is a sort of social and political half-authoritarian system—but disguised as a democracy—where the military often have a significant influence.

In the rhetoric of the day the terms market economy and democracy are used as if they were synonymous or at least naturally emerging at the same time. But this is wrong— or at least misleading. When the market economy or capitalism finally established itself in the 1800s and came to characterize modern industrial civilisation, democracy was at best in its infancy. In fact one could argue that democracy grew out of the contradictions and social dynamism inherent in the market economy of the capitalistic system. In this century we have a long list of terrifying and repressive regimes which have nevertheless upheld the virtues of a market economy. That some of these regimes have for ideological and security reason been hailed as bastions against communism, and also dignified members of the so-called free world does not transform them into demoeracies. In this company it is perhaps unnecessary to remind ourselves that the colonial system was assuredly not democratic, but was certainly based on capitalistic or market economic principles. It is the sad but irrefutable historical coupling between

Western democracy, colonialism, and the plundering of resources in the name of the market economy which for understandable reasons meant that many of the leaders of national liberation movements looked for other models for the development of their young nations. In this connection it can be worth remembering what Nelson Mandela said soon after his release from 26 years of prison in the market economic but racist state of South Africa. "When we in ANC during 40 years struggled for democracy we were put in prison by the same people who are now telling us how we should behave to promote the democracy we have been rejected by all these years".

While we can see that a market economy does not automatically lead to democracy, a functioning democracy— as we have defined it—does seem to require some form of free economic system.

Democracy and Economic Freedom

Theoretically, it is conceivable that a political democracy could be combined with an economy totally controlled by the government—but experience has shown this to be very difficult. One could even argue that it is by definition impossible since democracy implies a certain freedom of economic choice and independent economic actors. A functioning democratic system presupposes what is now often referred to as a civil society—in practice, independent institutions, companies, organisations, the media etc., regulated by law but not subject to or controlled by those in power.

We must also see clearly that there are no unambiguous relations between economic growth, development and democracy. Democratic governments are neither very successful when it comes to structural reforms which may be to the disadvantage of important interests in the society, nor when it comes to welfare. The developing countries which have achieved the greatest success economically and socially over the last 20 years are the East Asian countries—which all have had various kinds of more are less authoritarian systems.

However, that does not mean that you can use these countries as models for the rest of the world. There is no globally valid link between an authoritarian form of regime and economic development, not even when development is defined only in terms of autocentric growth. Many social scientists have tried to find some systematic connection between what we call development or modernisation on the one hand, and the political system on the other, but all have failed.

It is also obvious that one of several pre-requisites for economic growth and development is legitimate and reasonably well functioning government and governance. If the free market is to be a motor for development and improved welfare, and not just a meeting place for robber barons, the mafia and speculators, you must have a regulating and supportive state. If economic history teaches us anything, it is just this. Consider the astounding development in Germany after the war, or in Japan and the other East Asian countries some years later. There are many differences, but what they have in common is a well-functioning government apparatus with a long tradition.

Today we find ourselves in a historical situation where a large number of countries in the former communist states of Europe, in Africa, Asia and Latin America are at one and the same time trying to establish a new democratic system and new economic mechanisms. The situation is unique, and the intrinsic problems are unprecedented. Democracy as an idea has triumphed but in its practice it is in profound trouble. It is no exaggeration to talk of the crisis of democracy.

The former communist countries are certainly in crisis. As a by-product of the past regimes, there is an intensive suspicion of the political institutions, of the state and the parties, and in this way also the legitimacy of democracy and the ability of the politicians to deal with the fundamental problems of society has been undermined. The lack of a democratic tradition is not overcome from one day to the next.

Many of the developing countries have similar difficulties. The introduction of a multiparty system does not in itself mean that one can manage the conflicts and social problems in a democratic way.

Countries in Transition

Both in the East and the South countries are trying, at one and the same time, to change the political and economic system. When the whole society is convulsed by economic changes, and where peoples' living conditions fundamentally change, it is not easy to develop and maintain a political system based on compromise and respect, including respect for minorities.

As in previous history the deep crises of legitimacy and general frustration feed national and ethnical conflicts. These conflicts establish themselves in societies where the authoritarian system, economic crises and the break down of traditional values rob people of any kind of kinship other than ethnical.

We cannot avoid seeing disturbing signs of this crisis of democracy also in the so-called "established democracies" of the rich countries.

It is obvious that the state of democracy varies from country to country, as do the reasons for a feeling of dejection. But there are some similarities too.

The continuing and noticeable internationalisation limits the national freedom of political choice, available alternatives, and makes it more difficult for people to see the connection between "politics" and their actual living conditions. The governments are restrained by international economic events. The reaction of the stock exchange may be more important than that of the voters. The election results influence the stock exchange prices, but is it perhaps not also so that the stock exchanges, indirectly, also influence the election results? People feel themselves to be the victims of major economic changes, but no one seems to be responsible and they themselves feel they have little chance of influencing the outcome. The absence of clearly identifiable alternatives between the larger political parties provides opportunities for the populists and the extremists.

There is indeed reason to reflect on the lessons of the history of our turbulent and cruel century.

Priority for Growth

There is today much concern about the lack of resources for such urgent needs as the reconstruction of the fast, a concerted attack on poverty and human development in the poorest countries, and environmental investments of all kinds. If the growth of world output returns to the levels of the 1980s, total output would grow by about one trillion dollars a year. There is, in fact, no other way to resolve the economic and political crises multiplying in the world community than to give priority to the restoration of growth.

We are certainly not at the end of history as someone has argued. We are rather at a dramatic turning point, a moment of many possibilities and many dangers. What we do now, for a few years ahead, may direct the future for several decades—like the dramatic and fateful years immediately after the second world war. All nations, all governments, have a responsibility. The rich world has a special responsibility, not just moral because of its enormous economic and political power.

❋ ❋ ❋

24

Consuming the Future

Now that we are to reach six billion of us, it is a good point to check again on what sort of lifestyles we pursue and what is the environmental impact of those lifestyles. It is curious that we have spent several decades being concerned about the growing numbers of humankind while not giving at least an equal amount of attention to the levels of living we aspire to, and how many natural resources we chew up thereby and how much pollution and waste we cause.

Everybody is a consumer of sorts. True, every fifth person scarcely qualifies for that designation, consuming goods worth less than $1 per day. Conversely, every seventh person qualifies for a designation of super-consumer, with a cash income at least fifty times greater. These latter are the people who, through their carbon-di-oxide emissions, are disrupting everybody's climate dozens of times more than the average citizen of One Earth. Fair play, anyone?

Much as the have-nots seek to match the have's, it is plain their efforts will not work out for a long time to come, at best. If every Chinese person were to consume just one additional chicken per year and if the said chicken were to be raised primarily on grain, this would account for as much grain per year as all the grain exports of the number two exporter, Canada. If the Chinese were to raise their per capita consumption of beef, now only 4 kgs per year, to that of Americans, 45 kg, and if the additional beef were produced largely in feedlots after the manner of the United

States, it would account for as much extra grain as the entire US grain harvest, less than one-third of which is exported. Because of its recent climbing up the food chain toward a meat-based diet, China has become one of the world's leading importers of grain. The global grain market today is around 200 million tons per year, and shows scant scope for significant increase.

As a further measure of its ambitions, the Chinese government has designated the auto industry as one of five industry "pillars". Today China has fewer cars than Los Angeles. If per capita car ownership, together with oil consumption, were to match that of the United States, China would need 80 million barrels of oil per day—by contrast with the world's 1996 oil output of 64 million barrels of oil per day. The surge in carbon-di-oxide emissions would be unprecedented.

All this notwithstanding, there are already some 250 million newly affluent people in China. They are people with a household income equivalent to perhaps US $20,000, and enough discretionary income to enjoy the perquisites of the good life as perceived by these nouveaux riches. Top of the shopping lists are meat and more meat, followed by cars whether big or small. These are the badges of success: they show you have arrived.

The new consumers in China are matched by at least 200 million in India, and tens of millions in South Korea, Taiwan, Malaysia and Thailand (the recent economic setbacks have not permanently punctured the economic bubbles). Then there are 200 million more in Brazil, Argentina, Venezuela and Mexico, and more again in Hungary and other countries of Eastern Europe, also Turkey. Put them all together and they total about as many as the 800 million long established consumers in the ultra rich countries (the OECD grouping). When the current economic hiccups in Asia are left behind, the ranks of the new consumers can be expected to rise rapidly.

But they cannot hope to become super consumers. Where would all the extra gain come from? How could the global climate tolerate the huge additional pulse of carbon-di-oxide? There are all kinds of other environmental reasons to suppose that environmental constraints will become all the more constraining. True, technology could help moderate the environmental impact. We could enjoy twice as much material prosperity while using only half as much natural resources and causing half as much pollution and waste. But the new consumers will want to pursue the American dream to the hilt, and it is hard to see that the best technologies could enable huge numbers of affluent aspirants, perhaps two billion people by 2010, enjoying even half the material prosperity of Americans with average household incomes of $40,000.

But is it true "prosperity"—mental and emotional as well as material? Or is the American dream becoming a nightmare with its harried lifestyles and declining leisure time, where the shopping mall is the ultimate mecca, and the good life is a case of piling up goodies?

In any case, we cannot expect the new consumers to forego their "rightful share" of affluence unless the long-time affluent agree to cut back on their environmental ruinous lifestyles. It is these communities that must offer a strong example, and soonest. Where is the political leader who will espouse the new vision, however much it may be perceived as the ultimate vote loser?

25

What was Wrong with Structural Adjustment
In Defence of a Much-Maligned Strategy

After decades of stranded development theories, ideologies and paradigms, "structural adjustment", with its demands for clean fiscal policy and an end to uneconomic state enterprises, political privileges, market and exchange rate intervention and corruption, entered the aid arena like a refreshing dawn after a long night of frustrating dreams. Only the "old guard" of planned economy advocates and jealous academicians who had missed the boat were able to shut their eyes to the moral and economic justification of this liberating breakthrough in international development policy spearheaded by the Bretton Woods institutions then steered by some exceptionally courageous economists.

Reaction to SAPs

As with any revolution, defeat is awaiting the pioneers at the hands of political power greed, reactionary tactics by the formerly privileged and academic envy. The principal device serving the reactionary forces as a lever of influence on the mood of the "development community" has been the identification and dramatisation of new pockets or strata of (principally urban) poverty allegedly created by structural adjustment measures, while shunning the much broader-based rise in economic activity, real incomes and sense of fair reward in the overall society, especially the rural population. That the hardship experienced by urban poor, formerly privileged under consumer price control and import subsidies to the debit depressed farm prices or maintained by grossly over-expanded public payrolls, was only laying open the camouflaged erosion of the economy and near-bankruptcy of governments and public enterprises was conveniently downplayed.

These reactionary howls were to be expected. Not that they met the entirely innocent. There had been naively sweeping, overly assuming demands by some structural adjustment missions. But an intellectually vigorous and dynamic "development community" would have coped with the ensuing opposition, strengthened the analytical and monitoring capacities and the political will to endure also rocky roads and bitter medicines on the way to a healthier base. Instead, institutional rivalry, political opportunism and emotive populism were thriving. In a way, the "development community" behaved as if it did not want its patient to become able to stand on his own feet and eventually steal its raison d'être.

Worst, the Bretton Woods institutions themselves, partly under the pressure of the emotive opposition, described above, fell to the temptation to rescue their lending volume, which was threatened by the frugality dictated to Third World public budgets under structural adjustment recipes, through hardship-easing loans. They thereby corrupted their creation in using it to reinforce their indispensability. As a consequence it soon turned out that some of the most obedient loan takers under structural adjustment terms experienced sharply rising indebtedness, exploited as a disqualifying symptom by the anti-structural adjustment camp.

Whatever the opinions on structural adjustment policies, the commitment to the principles of "good governance" has come to stay, at least on paper, as an almost standard conditionally for official development aid from OECD donor countries. The realisation, matured in the implementation of structural adjustment programmes, that not the quantity of aid, but the quality of Third World governments determines the positive or negative course of development, may be regarded as the most valuable fruit of the decades-old policy debate in the 'development community". And the use of aid as a pressure or bribing factor towards "good governance" as foreign aid's least disputable purpose.

Out of the Limelight

Nothing, however, must be taken for granted. Achievement breeds its challenge! Structural adjustment, though in essence hardly disputable has been pushed out of the limelight and replaced by the oldest actor in the company: eradication of poverty, twinned with an equally perpetual endeavour at the macro-level: debt-forgiveness. This falling back to square one in donors' approach to the problems of the south, i.e., the call to alleviate poverty and priorities direct efforts to this end above all other developmental efforts— does it indicate a sell-out of constructive ideas in the "development community"? Has any noteworthy progress been achieved in the past by this approach?

By telling a frugally toiling but independent subsistence farmer that internationally his condition is classed as "poverty", deserving compassion and support by the world community and cancellation of his debts, one can hardly expect a sustainable improvement in his output, satisfaction, or self-respect and even less, when he realises that the help principally provides jobs, fringe benefits and self-importance to a gamut of intermediaries, at home and abroad.

What do those poverty advocates (the "Lords of poverty") really know about the resources, life managements, value systems and ambitions of those they generalise by the billions? The great variance in the conception of life situations, from different external viewpoints.

What the aid system can do for these rural populations classed as "poor"/"underprivileged"/"exploited", is press for justice, i.e., "good governance". The achievements of structural adjustment policy through, e.g. abolishing official price and exchange rate distortions, import subsidies and exploitative state agencies, has brought massive income improvement for peasant populations, i.e. the majority of LDC inhabitants, in dimensions unreachable by whatsoever direct "attack" on rural "poverty". What people want is not being benevolently treated as poor, but being justly rewarded for their work, i.e., by access to the unmanipulated market value of their output. Slackening on structural adjustment/"good governance" conditionally under the present "10 year itch" for paradigm change means foregoing much of the potential opportunities for undoing injustice and exploitation of the masses. It should be clear where priority focus should be placed in ODA policy.

Small is not Beautiful

The direct attack on "poverty", orchestrated by the Bretton Woods institutions under their freshly launched Poverty Reduction Strategy Paper (PRSP) campaign, is being rightly regarded as primarily an NGO domain, since most activities are expected to be carried out at local community level. This would require careful screening and coordinating of NGO activities and their integration via gradual expansion of their experience. But "small" is not "beautiful" for the development financing institution. Disbursement needs are pressing, calling for the new paradigm to quickly provide channels for another wave of loans to the "IDA Countries". Their problem of heavy indebtedness, which would principally exclude most of them from any new loan consideration, shall be solved with one stroke (which only the well-cushioned development bureaucracy can afford); debt relief against presentation of country PRSPs by the respective governments. NGOs are expected to play in the system especially the knowledge gap about the "poor" people's real wants and needs NGOs will naturally be tempted by such expansionary boost to their involvement (referred to sarcastically as their philanthropic empire" by an African conference participant), but this will not be conducive to quality and accountability of their performance, which ideally should be based on private sponsorship in combination with strong target-group provided self-help components.

Patience and Self-Restraint

Local knowledge and initiatives cannot be obtained under time pressure. "The grass does not grow faster by being pulled". When will the "development community" learn patience and self-restraint in the approach to LDC's capacity for constructive absorption of aid programmes accompanied by a genuine sense of ownership?

After all these deliberations, how shall development policy be shaped in order to better correspond with reality, without sinking deeper into hypocrisy and frustration?

To come back to the opening question: what was wrong with "structural adjustment"? Nothing was wrong with its intent. In fact this was very right and long overdue. Its implementation, however, lacked patience, perseverance and solid support from the development community, apart from its being corrupted as a vehicle for expansionary lending policy. If aid is meant to not be an end in itself, then structural adjustment policy needs constant reinforcement, underpinned by strict lending discipline. There should be an end to irresponsible lending and easy escape from its consequences by wholesome periodic debt relief burdened on the international tax-paying community. No ODA, either loans or grants, should be made available to governments who are not in active process of implementing "good governance" principles. A monitoring unit, reporting to the donor community on government performance in regard to its "good government"? Structural adjustment commitment, should be maintained in each and receiving country by "donor consortia" comprising all locally represented bilateral and multilateral development organisations currently extending technical, financial or material assistance to the country.

In order to accommodate the poverty focus without diluting the necessary structural adjustment orientation of ODA, a division of activity-focus between the latter and the NGO sector would seem to be advantageous.

- ODA, limited to the countries abiding to structural adjustment/"good governance" conditionally, with focus concentration on sustainable physical, social and economic infrastructure principally at national and regional level, public management training, higher education and research, consultant and senior adviser services.

- The NGO sector, principally funded by private sponsorship, united to structural adjustment conditionally (but preferably grafted on local self-help initiative), with focus-concentration on the "Third World "poor", i.e., mostly at rural community and low-income township level, for amelioration of living conditions and local resource utilisation.

- Strengthening of linkages between the NGO sector and the UN Technical Agencies to mutual benefit: NGOs in need of professional information, evaluation and advice or forum for discussion to find an actively supportive window at the agencies; the latter to maintain and develop field contact of research and policy generation, not least as a substitute for their declining project work (giving way to greater concentration on their global functions, i.e., serving as information, policy initiation, and coordination/negotiation centre on topics of global concern, such as e.g., human rights, global monetary and trade systems, tropical forest and global marine resources, global and regional health threats, international standards).

In conclusion, it may be called to mind that aid and its institutions have no claim for permanence. They are justified only as temporary functions in a phasing-out process of self-help support. Any claim for unlimited continuity would breed lasting infantilisation.

✳ ✳ ✳

26

World Trade—The Next Challenge

On 15 December 1993 the world changed. May be not as dramatically as the moment when the Berlin Wall fell, but then unlike that very necessary demolition job, the success of the Uruguay Round was a work of construction. Like the destruction of the wall, though, its effects will be profound and lasting ones felt far beyond its immediate context. It will be seen as a defining moment in modern history.

The importance of the Round can be seen in terms of boost it gives to job creation; to development; to investment; to economic reform; to the rule of law and in many other ways besides. All of these benefits are real and important. But the true value of the whole is much, much more than the sum of these parts.

Put simply, governments came to the conclusion that the notion of a new world order was not merely attractive but absolutely vital; that the reality of the global market—whatever ambitions some of them may retain for regional integration—required a level of multilateral cooperation never before attempted.

No Losers in the Round

It has created a revolutionary framework for economic, legal and political cooperation. But now turn to the immediate results of the Round. Seeing them as a profit and loss account or a scorecard of winners and losers is to see them in static terms, as one-off conclusions with finite effects. This misses the point completely.

Every nation now needs an effective trading system, but especially so the small and poor. They have it. Everyone will also gain from the huge package of market access results even if they did not get every concession they were seeking from trading partners—it is the biggest market access deal ever negotiated.

However, the essence of the Uruguay Round's achievements is that they are dynamic. The new agreements, the new rules and structures it sets up—all mean a commitment to a continuing process of cooperation and reform of which the agreement in December was only the beginning.

Maintaining the liberalising momentum will call for continuing effort and vigilance by participating countries. But now their energy can be focused through the Round's greatest innovation; the new World Trade Organisation (WTO) in place of the improvised basis on which the GATT has operated for 45 years, trade will now have a permanent forum appropriate to its importance in the world economy.

Technically speaking, the WTO will oversee the implementation of the Round's results, administer all the agreements in goods, services and intellectual property, and manage the unified dispute settlement system. But beyond these administrative functions, it will raise the political profile of trade a profile which has already been lifted greatly by the Uruguay Round. The WTO will have regular instead of occasional—direct Ministerial involvement. It will have a clear mandate to act as a forum for further trade negotiations. Most of all it will complete the transition from a trading system which largely restricted itself to policies at the border to one which also covers most aspects of domestic policy-making affecting international competition in goods and services, as well as investment.

Through the WTO, the Round will change the way the world economy is shaped. But it is not the final victory over protectionism and unilateralism. Any premature rejoicing would have quickly been cut short by the evidence since 15

December that major economic powers are still ready to take the unilateral approach to trade problems. Arguments for protectionism based on the alleged threat of low-cost competition to production and jobs will not just fade away because the Round is a success. The seductive appeal of "beggar-thy-neighbour" policies is highlighted by the seemingly greater vigour of the lobbies for protectionism than the advocates of open markets.

These dangers—and the speed with which they have resurfaced—make the achievement of the Uruguay Round all the more important, and its successful implementation all the more urgent. Implementation requires more than mutual backslapping about what we have achieved. It requires now that the US, EU and Japan, in particular, rapidly obtain final authority to ratify and also take a lead in providing the WTO with the means to fulfil its mandate.

The success of the Round has come at a time when it is even more vitally needed than anyone could have guessed when it was launched in 1986. Old structures and alignments have been turned inside out in trade as in every other area of international relations. We face a world of change and challenge, in which the reinforced trading system will be a primary source of stability and security.

The developing countries including India have become enthusiastic supporters of the multilateral trading system and the Uruguay Round even if all their demands were not met by industrial countries. The reasons lie in the changing economic policies of many developing countries and the clearer appreciation of the value of the GATT system that has grown along with these changes.

The challenge of new issues in world trade will be a major one for the WTO. The new organisation has to consider issues such as the links between trade and the environment, international competition policy, trade and investment, and trade and labour standards. To say a few words about trade and the environment since it is one area in which GATT member countries have committed themselves already to a comprehensive new work programme. They decided on 15 December, in conjunction with the adoption of the results of the Uruguay Round negotiations, to draw up a work programme on trade and environment by the Ministerial meeting in Marrakesh. Environmental policy-making is one of the most rapidly evolving areas of national and international policy-making, and it is entirely appropriate that emphasis should be placed now in GATT/WTO on ensuring better policy coordination and multilateral cooperation over the linkages between trade and environment.

Permanent Negotiations

The Uruguay Round may well be the last of its kind, but this in no way means the end of multilateral trade negotiations. On the contrary, it means they become a permanent event. Ad hoc negotiating rounds were necessary mainly because the GATT lacked the mandate or the institutional basis to operate the multilateral system to the full on a continuous basis. Between rounds the GATT has tended to lose momentum, often at the very times when it was essential to make the most of the liberalising impulse. This has allowed protectionism and unilateralism to recover and regroup and meant that each round has to start by regaining lost ground.

The positive results of the Uruguay Round will redefine much more than assumptions about trade. If they are exploited with the same determination, courage and commitment that went into concluding the Round, they should mean nothing less than a new start for sustainable growth and a new system of collective economic security for the world.

But if the trading system is now up to the job of supporting multilateral cooperation on such a wide scale, do the other structures of economic cooperation still meet the bill? The establishment of the WTO will put trade and investment on a par—perhaps rather in advance—of cooperation in monetary and financial areas. The WTO will stand alongside its original Bretton Woods sisters, the IMF and the World Bank. The three institutions must learn to work together even more effectively and closely. For example, rather than each body conducting separate reviews of country policies, is there not a case to be made for a more integrated approach on country reviews? But that does not, on its own, add up to effective multilateral economic cooperation. The question really has to be asked seriously: are the G7, the OECD, the regional groupings adequate to provide that cooperation?

It is the next challenge of international economic leadership—the challenge of translating the common interest in global growth into a practical and effective mechanism for solving our common economic problems together. So, the Ministers meeting in Marrakesh is an historic event which will establish the World Trade Organisation and put in place the new multilateral trading system, they will be making not an end, but a beginning.

✳ ✳ ✳

27

Asian Values Versus Western Democracy
The Pressures of Modernisation

Democracy in Asia is different from Western models. Often, it is only on paper while real power is wielded by autocratic governments. But with the growing integration into the world economy and rising prosperity, the people in Asia are demanding more participation and democratic freedoms.

Democracy has become a talking point also in Asia. Both within and outside the region, more and more people are asking if democracy as the prevailing political system and way of life could not be realised there, too. If it has taken Asia quite a while to get a debate on democracy underway, there are at least two reasons for the delay. First, initial approaches to democracy suffered a setback with the bloody crushing of the Chinese students' movement of Beijing's Tiananmen Square in 1989. That blow also affected the democracy movement beyond China's borders, and it is only gradually recovering from it. Second, the social preconditions for democratic development must, of course, be created. But apparently that is increasingly being done.

Democracy is certainly already a common political system in Asia. India is regarded as the world's biggest democracy. Democracy as a way of choosing the government and participation of the people in political decisions is also at least formally in place in Sri Lanka, Pakistan, the Philippines, Thailand, South Korea, Japan and Mongolia.

Even in Singapore, Malaysia and Indonesia, the regimes seek to legitimise their political systems as independent, 'non-western' forms of democracy. So there is no simple answer to the question of democracy in Asia. A number of factors have to be taken into account.

Democracy and Culture

Asia is not only the world's biggest and most populous continent, but also has its greatest cultural, religious and linguistic disversity. The debate on whether Asia is capable of democracy must therefore include the cultural aspect in particular. And that calls for getting to grips with many cliches and prejudices. One of the best-known cliches, trotted out by politicians and intellectuals both within and outside the region, is the assertion that Asia's different quality of life stands in the way of introducing the 'western' concept of democracy there. The prime ministers of Singapore and Malaysia, as well as, of course, the Chinese leadership, have long lauded 'Asian values'. They say these values are fundamentally opposed to the western concept of government and society, which is why the latter could not be realised in an Asian context. The American political scientist Samuel Huntington reinforced this line with his projection of a coming 'clash of cultures'. But no matter how prominent its proponents are they do not give the assertion any more credence. Not least in Asia itself, more and more voices revealed the touting of 'Asian values' to be the attempt to ruling elites to safeguard their power and deny the people political participation.

At any rate, democracy can also in Asia be defined in terms of international and now widely accepted criteria in the sense of a liberal political system. That concrete implementation and building of institutions must respect local conditions is not disputed. A look at Asian culture shows that roots for democracy are most certainly to be found in the region. The South Korean politician Kim Dae Jung, for example, cites tenets of ancient Chinese philosophy which said the will of the people must be understood and respected as the will of Heaven. Individual rights to freedom are certainly compatible with Chinese culture. True, it would be going too far to interpret Confucianism as a source of democratic ideals. But there is no doubt that in its cognitive and ehtical systems classiçal Confucianism was a culture of learning, rationality and justice.

This is the foundation of what is probably the most stable democracy in Asia, that of Japan. There, a kind of philosophical pragmatism linked harmoniously the traditions of Confucianism, Buddhism, Shintoism and Christianity to form the base on which to build a new 'state philosophy'. And even in India, with its great ethnic and cultural diversity, the Westminster model of parliamentary democracy is linked without difficulty with the tradition of Hinduism. Thus, it is possible to connect the caste system, despite all its blatant social injustice, with a political culture which places remarkably great importance on holding elections. In Pakistan and Bangladesh, democratic processes have not only been introduced in Islamic countries, but especially surprisingly—their first democratic governments were led by women. That is also a telling argument against the Asian culture cliche. The case of South Korea shows in turn how in a relatively short period, transparency of government action, growing influence of public opinion, women's access to work, and independence of the judiciary have become established as largely acknowledged standards. In Europe, that took centuries.

In addition, the recent history of Asian countries has not indicated that striving for harmony and shunning disobedience, dissent and conflict are fixed elements of Asian culture. From the turn of the century, there was growing resistance against the colonial powers and local rulers in India, China, former Malaya, Indonesia and elsewhere in the region. And right up to the 1960s there were in many places strong Communist parties or movements which staged protests upto military action both inside and outside their countries. Authoritarian regimes instrumentalise the Asians' alleged need for harmony for ideological purposes. And some western observers readily fall for that subterfuge out of laziness or ignorance.

Economy and Democracy

The transformation processes of the last decade have shown that the reasons for a change of political system and the stabilisation of democracy are many-sided, and can differ from country to country. For example, economic declilne or success can lead equally to democracy or the shattering of it. Contrary to the earlier assumptions of democratic modernisation, we now know that successful economic development is not necessarily a precondition for democracy. In Asia, that is shown quite clearly by the examples of the Philippiness and Monogolia, where turning to democracy appeared to be the way out of a desperate economic situation. On the other hand, the cases of South Korea and Taiwan prove that in the wake of economic improvement more and more people prefer a democratic system, more personal freedom and chances of political participation. The reverse appears to be the case in Singapore, Malaysia and Indonesia, because economic growth there was accompanied by a consolidation of authoritarian structures or establishment of merely formal democracies. The two most stable democracies in Asia are Japan and India.

Supports of Democratic Development

Democracy everywhere needs classes of supporters that stimulate political change and stand in the wings as an alternative government. In Asia, there is now broad agreement that in social market economy countries, economic modernisation leads to a differentiation in their societies that is a precondition for pluralism and democratic development. Above all, the emergence and strengthening of an urban middle class in the Asian democracies is of great significance. But the upper class also plays an important role in enabling democracy. Thus, democratic stability in Thailand depends to a great degree on the government and upper class coming to terms with each other, as well as inclusion of the middle class in the political process. In Thailand, and also in the Philippines, Taiwan and South Korea, democratisation was accompanied by economic liberalisation and cutbacks in government regulation of commerce and industry. It was probably no coincidence that in these countries the economic structural adjustment process of the beginning of the 1980s was followed by a wave of democratisation, which surged from the end of the decade. As in Thailand, Taiwan's focus on exports triggered the rise of small and medium-sized enterprises and a gradually strengthening middle class.

In contrast, commerce and industry in Singapore, Malaysia and Indonesia is subject to considerable government control. If the middle classes which emerged on the back of these countries' economic development fail to call for political participation, that is certainly not only because their governments fulfill their expectations on distribution, convincingly portray the ruling systems as 'authentic democracy' and are skilful in mobilising resentments against alleged destabilisation attempts by the 'West'. Rather, the upper class and the new middle classes also remain politically weak because transformation to the market economy is greatly dependent on government investment. They cannot take on the role of promoters and supporters of democratisation. Where pro-democratic forces are vulnerable to a government's many options of applying sanctions, they remain weak. If the government, as in Singapore, controls 90 per cent of the housing market, rules society with a firm hand, and has a decisive influence on commerce and industry, there are few possibilities of escaping the grip of repression by seeking refuge in a private sector.

The situation is similar in Malaysia and Indonesia, where the weakness of the middle class is linked with the fact that most graduates of senior high schools and universities take jobs in the public sector. In Indonesia, the Pancasila ideology of national unity in proving less and less suited to establish social cohesion. The country's entrepreneurs depend to a great degree on government business. In political terms, compared with the Sukarno family's plutocracy they play only the role of 'substitute capitalists'. However, events in South Korea and Taiwan, whose regimes have indeed long been legitimised essentially only by their economic performance, suggest that it is not possible to repress social pluralism and growing demands for participation in the long term.

A strengthening of civil society organisations has been noted in many Asian countries in recent years. It would certainly not be too bold to forecast that these organisations will promote not only economic liberalisation, but also political opening. The nation-wide trade union strike actions in South Korea at the turn of this year were a clear signal in this direction. They proved that pressures for more participation and better social and working conditions increase along with economic growth. The countries of Southeast Asia must expect something similar, which is why some still shy away from further political liberalisation.

In Singapore, Malaysia and Indoneisa, an additional factor hinders the development of democracy. It is one which in probably no other Asian country, except perhaps for India, carries so much weight. This is the multi-ethnic composition of their societies and its associated potential for conflict. The elites of these countries fear ethnic or religious clashes that could have destabilising impacts. However, it is uncertain how long a certain ethnic group can asset a claim to sole power. That applies, for example, to the bumiputras, the 'Sons of the Earth' in Malaysia. In India, not even the caste system can guarantee the Brahmins their privileged status for ever. In this context, the Philippines government has drawn attention in recent years. It has not only linked economic prosperity with political liberality, but also peacefully settled its conflict with the Moslem minority on Mindanao and integrated them in the pluralistic and democratic state system.

Weak Democratic Institutions

In many Asian countries, democratic institutions are so far only weakly developed. There are in many places only the beginnings of a functioning separation of powers. Parliaments are often almost without significance in the face of strong presidents or bureaucracies. The judiciary is often subject to direct government influence, and corruption is a widespread evil. Even in the established democracies of India and Thailand, massive buying of votes is routine. True, there are now multi-party system in most countries of the region. But, except mainly for India and Japan, the parties are weak on organisation and often aligned more on a charismatic leader than on a programme.

China and Indochina

Although the Chinese and Vietnamese Communist Party congresses in the autumn of this year, particularly Beijing's took more strides towards economic opening, they confirmed forecasts that political doors would remain closed. Only the beginnings of a civil society or expectations of political participation can be noted there. In Vietnam, for example, there have been indications of the emergence of forms of civil society organisations since the regime realised that the state alone cannot provide the necessary development inputs. In addition, with their opening to foreign investment, new legal structures have begun to develop in both countries which hold out the long-term prospect of winning room for manoeuvre from the state" arbitrary rule.

On the other hand, the case of Cambodia shows how difficult it is to introduce democracy after 20 years of civil war if the social prerequisites for it have not yet been created. The brutalising of political culture, a poor level of education, immense social and economic problems, antagonistic political structures, and anyway, the absence of a supporting class, greatly impedes democratic development. That certainly also applies to Burma.

Eternal Demands for Democracy?

Unlike other regions, the robust self-confidence of the Asian tiger economies and their lesser dependence on western development assistance leads them to reject external demands for democratic processes and organisations to be established in non-democratic countries as undesired interference in their internal affairs. Japan, the region's largest donor and investor, has in any case no such ambitions. Nevertheless, in most Asian countries there are signs of a growing interest in a socio-political dialogue and exchange of experience. The mechanisms of the past are increasingly being differentiated for organisational purposes, and complex societies are apparently more and more being perceived as insufficient. New social issues in the context of economic modernisation, new security policy tasks in the shadow of China's growing military strength, and new environmental burdens are sparking increasing interest in an international exchange of experience. The continuing economic prosperity that Asian countries are expected to enjoy, at least in the medium term, and their further integration in the world market will probably fuel even more their people's expectations of political participation, thus also promoting the development of democracy.

28

The Trade Related Intellectual Property Rights (TRIPS) Agreement and the Developing Countries

The basic norms of free competition established in the nineteenth century induced legislators to provide relatively weak forms of intellectual property protection. Often innovators could rely only on such factors as lead time, reputation for quality and continuing technical improvements to maintain their foothold in the market.

Undermining this outlook were two developments that led to the inclusion of intellectual property issues in the World Trade Organisation (WTO). First, the rise of knowledge-based industries radically altered the nature of competition and disrupted the equilibrium that had resulted from more traditional comparative advantages. Second, the growing capacity of manufacturers in developing countries to penetrate distant markets for traditional industrial products forced the developed countries to rely more heavily on their comparative advantages in the production of intellectual goods than in the past. Market access for developing countries thus became a bargaining chip to be exchanged for greater protection of intellectual goods within a restructured global market place.

Since 1986 the developed countries' drive for extra-territorial protection of intellectual property rights has largely ignored the competitive capabilities of developing countries with respect to intellectual goods, and it has also downplayed these countries' rights to preferential treatment under existing rules. At the same time, the logic of multilateral trade negotiations skews the pre-existing North-South conflict over intellectual property rights by introducing the prospects of trade concessions in unrelated fields. Intellectual property rights constitute but one of many variables that bear on competitive capacity and the transfer of technology in general.

Primary Intellectual Property Regimes

Patents

The extension of patentability to virtually all types of technology recognised by developed patent systems, the prolongation of patent protection to a uniform term of twenty years, and legal recognition of the patentee's exclusive rights to import the relevant products could adversely affect developing countries whose existing patent laws fall below these standards. In practice, however, the competitive status of any given developing country in a post-TRIPS world will depend in part on the level of foreign direct investment it attracts and on the benefits that strengthened intellectual property rights bring to domestic innovators.

Competition under stronger patent regimes requires developing countries to adopt legal means of narrowing the scope of foreign patent monopolies and of encouraging local entrepreneurs either to work around the claimed inventions or to develop improvements suited to local conditions. To this end, local entrepreneurs should exploit technical information in disclosures published abroad; patent authorities should exercise all of the claims limitations practised abroad; and domestic courts should strictly interpret the doctrine of equivalents. Legislative enactments of utility model laws would provide additional incentives to adapt foreign inventions to local conditions and to improve them further.

Moreover, unpatented traditional technologies will often remain suitable for local needs, and the resulting products may be sold at lower prices than imported products of patented technologies. Entrepreneurs in developing countries should also be prepared to exploit unpatented applications of applied scientific know-how in such advanced technologies as biogenetic engineering and computer programme-related innovation.

In time, increased direct investment by foreign patentees could enable developing country licensees who exploit their natural advantages, especially low labour costs, to succeed on both domestic and export markets where non-licensees were unable or unwilling to venture in the past. Familiarisation with the benefits of the patent system should stimulate greater investment in domestic research and development and in technological innovation.

The gradual extension of patents to new technologies such as computer programmes and bio-genetic engineering without the emergence of agreed international minimum standards creates both opportunities and risks for the developing countries. While the developed countries enjoy unique advantages in biotechnology that only become available to developing countries as a consequence of stronger patent systems, some developing countries may find their own competitive status enhanced by the provision of proprietary rights, including plant breeders' rights, though others may not. The patenting of biogenetic advances decreases the scope for reverse-engineering and could also increase the costs of doing business in key sectors of some developing economies, notably agriculture. As regards information technologies, reliance on copyright and trade secrets at the international level appears less unfavourable to the developing countries' prospects than patents, for reasons that are set out below. However, the tendency to patent software could diminish these prospects by posing limits to reverse engineering and to the attainment of the interoperability, and this trend adds to the overall costs of disseminating information goods.

To the extent that patented technology is not made available on reasonable terms or that un-wholesome economic dependencies actually arise, developing countries will have to consider measures to restore the competitive balance that are consistent with the TRIPS agreement. For example, the agreement allows compulsory licences when the rights holders fail to licences patented technology "on reasonable commercial terms". It also provides other bases for defensive regulatory action by emphasising "the transfer and dissemination of technology, to the mutual advantage of producers and users" and the need "to promote the public interest in sectors of vital importance to socio-economic and technological development".

Measures to restrain abuses of intellectual property rights as authorised by the Paris Convention also remain available under the TRIPS agreement, which expressly empowers developing countries to deal with licensing practices that "adversely affect the international transfer of technology".

Finally, the agreement specifically preserves the right of all states to "adopt measures necessary to protect public health and nutrition and to promote the public interest in sectors of vital importance to socio-economic and technological development, provided that such measures are consistent with the provisions of this agreement".

Trademarks and Geographical Indications

The TRIPS provisions give pre-existing norms greater specificity while softening the use requirement and eliminating both compulsory licences and local linkage requirements. These provisions also subject the international regime of trade marks and unfair competition to more stringent enforcement measures, including border controls against imports of counterfeit goods.

As a result, developing countries will need to reassess the pro-competitive functions of trade marks in open economies while addressing questions of abuse in a more direct fashion. They should insist on receiving the technical cooperation and aid that the TRIPS agreement envisages for the purpose of defraying administrative and enforcement burdens.

Governments should consider policies and incentives that encourage enterprises to establish their own market identities through appropriate trade marks and foreign firms to allow licensees to adapt more of the licenced products for both domestic and export needs under local trade marks.

Copyrights

Authors in many developing countries are very active in both domestic and foreign markets. It nonetheless remains true that the balance of trade in cultural goods favours exports from developed countries. This imbalance could increase under the TRIPS agreement, which generally applies the international minimum standards of the Berne Convention, plus selected standards from the Rome Convention on neighbouring rights.

While efforts to implement these standards is mandatory, developing country authorities should familiarise themselves with the extent to which the scope of copyright protection varies from country to country, in the absence of authoritative legal limitations recognised by international law. Carefully framed public-interest exceptions may further reduce the overall costs of a TRIPS agreement without violating international copyright norms. Moreover, the revised Berne Convention already provides for compulsory licences for educational and scientific test, and developing countries may wish to consider making greater use of these concessions.

Ancillary Proprietary Regimes

Trade Secrets

In modern economies trade secret law regulates the pace of competition by endowing second comers with an absolute right to reverse-engineer. To operate successfully under such a regime, developing countries must realign the concept of "transfer of technology" with the nature of competition on open markets. Technology is transferred through self-help methods of reverse engineering. The potential benefits of reverse-engineering unpatented technologies increase when advanced technologies are involved, notably biogenetic engineering, computer programmes and computer-aided design. The unpatented, non-copyrightable know-how underlying these technologies is often embodied in tangible products available to the pubic, which renders classical trade secret protection of doubtful efficacy. By ignoring this problem, the TRIPS Agreement provides entrepreneurs in developing countries with major opportunities, notwithstanding the extension of trade secret law under TRIPS, provided they are willing and able to master the art of reverse-engineering.

Other Proprietary Regimes

The TRIPS Agreement mandates intellectual property protection for industrial designs, plant varieties and integrated circuit designs. Although the developed countries enjoy a clear advantage in advanced sectors of industrial design, more traditional sectors rooted in aesthetic appeal rather than technical efficiency remain accessible to firms in developing countries.

Need for Multilateral Policies

Global economic integration increasingly requires that intangible creations receive minimum international standards of legal protection. Purely territorial intellectual property rights will thus give way to international sovereignty. However, the norms, of that law represent a delicate balance between the interests of States at different stages of development, so that the evolution of international intellectual property law will have to accommodate these norms and that balance.

Efforts to implement higher intellectual property standards will put increasing strains on competition law, which is not directly covered by the TRIPS Agreement. Identifying the parameters of healthy competition valid for all players in an integrated world market will become a pressing task for the international community in a post-TRIPS world. These issues will be complicated by the fact that innovators, users, and second comers all have different stakes in fashioning the rules of unfair competition law, and their interests will increasingly vary more with their economic roles than with the geopolitical affiliations of their respective national States.

Competition law must, become an integral part of international discussions of intellectual property rights, and there is a great need for multilateral cooperation to achieve a marketwide balance between incentives to create, and reasonable opportunities to imitate and improve upon, technological innovation. These discussions should lead to an internationally agreed framework for promoting a transfer of technology that is compatible with the drive for greater economic efficiency. To the extent that such cooperation succeeds, it will contribute a new perspective to the notion of fair competition that should strengthen the prospects of all participants in the global marketplace.

✳ ✳ ✳

29

Markets Thrive on Information

Despite decades of structural adjustment pitched at freeing markets and years of policy emphasis on enabling small business, very many developing countries have suffered stagnating real incomes. Economic inertia is inevitable in any nation lacking functional business media. Journalists not only serve as public watchdogs in politics—they are also relevant for market efficiency.

In Ghana, five people died in riots triggered by the introduction of a value added tax in 1995. Imposed at the same rate and on the same products as the sales tax it was to replace, it was not a change that would morally have led to fighting in the streets. But journalists had got it wrong. According to their reports the tax would have drastically increased prices for consumers. In a country weary of painful structural adjustment policies, that was enough to trigger violence. But it wasn't true—the truth was that the journalists didn't understand the new tax. They had bought a line from interest groups that stood to lose out when the tax anomalies it was targeting were ended. Nonetheless, with the public at boiling point, the tax was abandoned.

This case was just one example of event caused by the lack of business journalism skills common to many emerging economies. It perfectly illustrates just how powerful business journalism can be. This event and many more like it prompted the World Bank, in 2002, to start training business journalists.

A Bridge for Public Understanding

While the watchdog role of political journalism is generally well understood, the similar role of business media has received very little attention in developing nations. Much emphasis has been placed on making financial decisions and transactions transparent. But that only helps to close down possibilities for graft, favour and simple incompetence when misbehaviour is made visible. Someone has to be watching, where data is produced that is read and understood by only a small circle of experts, transparency becomes at best accountability to powerful economic agents. There needs to be a bridge for public understanding.

A perfect example of this is currently unfolding in South Africa, where so called black economic empowerment (BEE) is driving a redistribution of wealth. Business media strongly support this politically correct trend. However, there are signs that the process is going seriously awry. This issue has been identified and even highlighted with data-rich press releases by financial experts. Nonetheless, the media have mostly ignored such information.

Last year, BEE drove a surge in merger and acquisition activity to a deal value of Rand 42.2bn. The business media reported this surge in strongly positive terms. Yet the data that gave this headline growth figure also highlighted that the majority of all of the country's BEE M&A deals were moving formerly white resources into the ownership of the black political elite: 60 per cent of the deals made in 2003 accrued to the companies of just two black politicians— Patrice Motsepe and Tokyo Sexwale.

This asset building by two men is far removed from the stated aims and ideals of black empowerment. Rather, it resembles the perversion of privatisation seen in almost all emerging economies from Russia outwards. Yet the business media in South Africa, instead of clamouring over such data, is close to silent. Reports are not even communicating the data neutrally, in order that readers can make their own judgements on whether this represents black empowerment.

Such situations show that transparency rules are of little use, unless active media are serving as watchdogs to alert the wider public. Distortions continue to occur under conditions of transparency unless they are reported. This, however, in not the worst damage resulting from poor media coverage.

Business media output, and the numbers of business journalists required to produce it, has burgeoned everywhere in the last two decades. A challenge exists across all nations in finding and retaining capable staff. They need to accept relatively moderate pay in spite of having the business and financial competence in huge demand throughout commerce.

The skills gap is far greater in development economies than in North America, western Europe or Japan. Business journalism entrants everywhere tend to be unfamiliar with the basic tenets of accounting, the financial markets, and economic relationships. But these skills are rarely present at any level of the profession in emerging economies. This results in business coverage primarily relaying headline growth figures with little explanation. It skirts detail, makes errors and is open to manipulation. Moreover, it fails to perform a series of functions vital to economic expansion and success.

Easily accesible business data tend to drive down consumer prices and to promote greater efficiency in processing and marketing. Competent media coverage contributes to making good strategic business decisions and helps to prevent business failures. All this adds up to more jobs and higher job security.

The Value of Comparative Data

In Kenya, in 1996, a group of journalists spent a collective 30 hours compiling a league table of interest rates on offer to Kenyan borrowers. Until then, the banks' loan rates and conditions had never been compiled and published. That is why the spread ran from 13 per cent to more than 30 per cent. Without information and comparison, there was

no need for banks to compete on price. Kenyan borrowers
took put luck-normally opting for the bank recommended by
a relative or neighbour or coincidentally close to an oft-used
thoroughfare. That was fine for anyone who stumbled across
a 13 per cent loan. But for the very many who were paying
25 to 33 per cent it meant disaster. Such interest payments
are tough on business anywhere. An initial lack of
information in an uncompetitive market can easily doom
projects to failure.

This lack of competition, rooted in an inefficient
information market, has severely hampered Kenya's small
and medium scale enterprise (SMEs). Nonetheless, the
business media did not start to publish comparative interest
rate offering on a continuous basis. Only years later, did the
central bank step in with a regular information feed on loan
interest rates which is now covered by the business press.
In most rich countries, media companies would not have
waited for such an official but would have gone on to research
and publish comparative data.

This kind of information is often peripheral for large
businesses, which have specialists dedicated to information
collection and decision-making. Giant corporations employ
lawyers, marketing managers, technical experts and other
professionals. They also spend liberally in the fee-paying
business information market, from market research reports
to consultancy services. Small companies cannot afford such
an effort for scanning their business environment. Yet the
success of small business is a precondition of an economy's
take-off.

In this US, small business produce more than half of
the nation's total output. They also employ the majority of
workers and create almost all of the country's net new jobs.
In Europe, the picture is similar, with a third of the western
European labour force in firms with less than 10 employees,
excluding farms. Nothing can compensate for the economic
gap created by a dormant or under-performing SME sector.
But to achieve small business vibrancy, two hurdles must be

overcome. Very many new businesses must be started, a significant proportion of which must succeed. In both areas, the business media plays a key role.

Support for Small Enterprises

To start new business, the economically active must understand entrepreneurship as a real and achievable option. People start business and it works. In the US a large slice of the business media is preoccupied with the realities of small business, carrying case studies and tales and experience. Consequently, running a small business is understood as an ever-present possibility.

Once small business emerges as a real option, the business media becomes essential in fuelling business expansion by signaling threats and highlighting opportunities. In the UK, where there are 10,000 business magazines and journals generating estimated annual revenues of more than 3.3bn, two-thirds of business people surveyed by the Periodical Publishers Association classified business magazines as essential reading. Across every sector and sub-sector, these publications serve to set up clubs and information networks, relaying market trends, technological data, job advertisements and information about competitors.

Marking business decisions without this kind of information represents a considerable handicap. In the UK, the Agridata Snapshot Readership Survey in 2002 found that 95 per cent of farmers read at least one farming publication. The majority of these same farmers also have Internet connection, and can access relevant information directly. The idea of a majority of Ghanian farmers being Internet connected and picking up US agricultural data, or information on the current Brazilian coffee harvest, and thus current coffee price trends, is close to absurd. It would, however, improve their business outlook. Entirely more viable is a single, capable agricultural publication to digest information relevant to farming in Ghana. Typically the business press should signal conferences, trade fair opportunities, buyers and sellers requirements, and, arriving at a low cover price, than pass on the information to a chain of many readers.

Similarly, radio in emerging markets has a reach and a capacity hardly ever deployed to relay relevant business news. Few journalists currently understand the importance of cash-flow. Yet between two-thirds and 90 per cent of new businesses fail because of cash-flow problems. This is surely reason enough to classify cash-flow management as a subject that deserves high attention even at the level of community radio.

More generally, it is hard to see how any industry without a forum used by all to advertise job vacancies can efficiently recruit appropriate personnel. Similarly, without a functioning business press, sliced around target audiences, small businesses are left with few ways of telling would-be customers that they exist. A flower producer cannot, with the single act of placing a cheap advertisement in the right business media, automatically reach flower buyers; an ingredients maker cannot affordably identify and reach a large line-up of food processors; a basketweaver cannot opt for a home improvement audience or the home improvement retail industry.

This loads market opportunities towards large, established, normally multi-national players. They can afford to spend heavily on advertising using billboards, national newspapers and broadcast media. African farmers might be able to source equipment locally, if they knew it was available. Instead the only equipment they know of is that which is backed by big marketing spends.

In the absence of a competent business press, the SME engine of economic growth remains hamstrung. Yet while the link between a competent mainstream media and democracy is accepted as a tenet of the current orthodoxy, there is in such understanding of the relationship between the business media and economic success.

✳ ✳ ✳

30

Climate Politics After Kyoto
Solidarity Understood Correctly

The Kyoto Protocol does not do enough to protect humankind from climate change. Additional binding reduction targets for greenhouse gases are necessary and they must also apply to important developing and transition countries. So far, these countries have been treated as a uniform group. In future, different rules will have to be used according to varying capabilities and different exposures to risk.

The Kyoto Protocol climate protection came into force internationally in February. At its core are binding commitments for industrialised countries to restrict their greenhouse gas emissions. This is an important step—however, it is only the first one in coming to terms with the challenge of the century: climate protection. The reduction targets of five per cent on average for advanced nations established so far are insufficient. Moreover, there are no obligations yet for developing and transition countries, which emit almost half of the greenhouse gases worldwide.

At the climate summit in Buenos Aires the European Union tried to kick-start negotiations on the further development of the Kyoto Protocol with moderate success. While the negotiations in the run-up to Kyoto were already quite difficult, the new phase of international climate politics that is just beginning presents even greater obstacles. Apart from reintegrating the climate—desperado USA into the international process, future negotiations will have to involve several transition and developing countries.

However, these countries point to the rich nations' historic responsibility for ongoing climate change. They are afraid their economic development might be slowed down. Meanwhile, many of the poorer developing countries are particularly vulnerable. Due to their geographical location, economic structure and weak financial and technical capacities, they are virtually, helplessly exposed to the consequences of the greenhouse effect. Therefore, future negotiations must break the "North - South" grid as well as find an adequate differentiation for the very heterogeneous countries of the "South".

The central theme of our work was the principle of solidarity. This implies that weak countries should be supported when tackling the effects of climate change. As started in Article 2 of the Framework Convention of Climate Change, humankind's "dangerous" interference with the climate must be stopped. This means that global warming must be restricted to, atmost, two centigrades above pre-industrial temperatures. Any warming above this level would threaten human existence in many regions. The cultural survival of local communities and the physical integrity of the weak and powerless would be acutely endangered.

Mitigation Becomes a Negotiation Topic

Even in keeping to this two degree mark, which the European union has adopted, impact of climate change, which is already noticeable now, would be aggravated further. The first conclusion of our team therefore is that future negotiations can no longer deal merely with combating the causes of the problem by reducing emissions. Talks have to go further and contribute to limiting damage. Measures to adapt to climate change, particularly in the case of very vulnerable countries, must play a central role.

In terms of finance, technology and personnel, many developing countries are in no position to adequately handle the negative consequences of climate change. They need transfer payments. Financing mechanisms that correspond to the "polluter pays" principle are inevitable—and introducing them is a precondition to move a head with preventive measures. Developing countries will only be prepared to accept reduction targets for emissions if the industrialised countries contribute (financially)to adapting to climate change. All summed up, however, reduction and prevention of greenhouse gases also serve adaptation programmes. The more effectively climate protection is implemented, after all, the lower the costs for adapting to the climate change will be—not to mention irreversible effects of climate change, such as the extinction of animal and plant species and the melting of glaciers.

If climate change is to be limited to two degrees Celsius on average globally humankind's emissions must peak by 2020, drop to half level reached in the 1990s by the middle of this century and then continue to decrease. There is widespread agreement among politicians, scientists civil society actors on the necessity of emission reductions the difficulties begin with question of which countries are to contribute. When does their obligation begin and what extent does it have?

The Kyoto Protocol retains the categories outlined in the Framework Convention on Climate Change. Accordingly, the advanced Western nations and the former Soviet block form one group (Annex countries) and the rest of the World the second group (Non-annex I countries). This is not practical in the long term.

The Kyoto Protocol defines negotiated reduction obligations among the parties of the first group. Given the increasing contribution of the "rest of the world" to global emission levels , future regulations must also engage several transition and developing countries. To do so, it is necessary to differentiate more strongly between these countries— according to their capabilities and circumstances.

Criteria for Differential Treatment

In order to reflect the country—specific conditions in a fair manner, our proposal consider three criteria:

* the potential to reduce greenhouse gases;
* the capacity to finance reduction measures; and
* the responsibility for climate change.

In view of these criteria, the Non-annex I countries obviously differ greatly. As a matter of course, all countries with the lowest emissions per capita are included. However, so are several countries with the highest emissions per capita world wide—Qatar,for example. All least developed countries (LDC) fall into the category, but so do countries such as Singapore, with a per capita income well above the average of the industrialised countries. Obviously, it does not make sense to treat these countries as equals in climate talks.

If the "Non-annex countries" are differentiated according to the three criteria mentioned above, four groups can be identified:

* "Newly industrialising countries" (NIC);
* Rapidly industrializing developing countries" (RIDC);
* Other developing countries" (ODC);
* "Least developed countries"(LDC).

COUNTRY GROUPS

Newly Industrialised Countries"—NICs

Bahrain, Brunei, Cuba, Kazakhastan, South Korea, Kuwait, Qatar, Saudi Arabia, Singapore, Suriname, Trinidad and Tobago, Turkmenistan, United Arab Emirates, Uzbekistan.

"Rapidly Industrialising Developing Countries"—RIDs

Algeria, Antigua and Barbuda, Argentina, Bahamas, Barbodos, Belize, Bosnia and Herzegovina, Botswana, Brazil,

Chile, China, Colombia, Costa Rica, Cyprus, Dominican Republic, El Salvador, Fiji, Grenada, Guyana, Iran, Jordan, Malaysia, Malta, Mauritius, Mexico, Oman, Panama, Peru, Philippines, Saint Kitts and Nevis, Saint Lucia, Saint Vincent and Grenadines, South Africa, Thailand, Tunisia, Uruguay.

Other Developing Countries—ODCs

Armenia, Azerbaijan, Bolivia, Cameroon, Congo, Cook Islands, Cote d'Iovire, Dominica, Ecuador, Egypt, Gabon, Georgia, Ghana, Honduras, India, Indonesia, Jamaica, Kenya, Kyrgyzstan, Libya, Macedonia, FYR, Moldova, Mongolia, Morocco, Namibia, Nicaragua, Nigeria, Pakistan, Papua New Guinea, Paraguay, Seychelles, Sri Lanka, Swaziland, Syria, Tajikistan, Venezuela, Vietnam, Zimbabwe.

Least Developed Countries—LDCs

Afghanistan, Angola, Bangladesh, Benin, Bhutan, Burkina Faso, Burundi, Cambodia, Cape Verde, Central African Republic, Chad, Comoros, Democratic Republic of Congo, Djibouti, Equatorial Guinea, Eritrea, Ethiopia, Gambia, Guinea, Guinea-Bissau, Haiti, Kiribati, Laos, Lesotho, Liberia, Madagascar, Malawi, Maldives, Mali, Mauritania, Mozambique, Myanmar, Nepal, Niger, Rwanda, Samoa, Sao Tome and Principe, Senegal, Sierra Leone, Solomon Islands, Somalia, Sudan Tanzania, Togo, Tuvalu, Uganda, Vanuatu, Yemen, Zambia.

We are not interested in splitting the negotiating group of the "G 77 and China" politically. But solidarity among these countries requires that those which are better off make a contribution to global climate protection on a different scale than, for example, the LDCs. Only in this way can the group retain its important unity in negotiations with the advanced countries and, at the same time, tackle the climate problem.

What would the climate protection obligations of the different country groups look like in concrete terms? We propose the following rules:

- The potential to reduce emissions should determine binding reduction targets. This potential arises from the emission intensity of a country (CO_2 emitted per unit of the gross domestic product) and from the emissions per capita. This line of action would guarantee a cost efficient climate regime, since emissions would be reduced wherever the potential for doing so was highest. This does not necessarily mean, however, that the countries, concerned would be liable to fund all necessary measures. Certainly the industrial countries would have to contribute too;

- Obligations to finance climate protection would have to derive from the respective capacity of a country. This capacity could be measured against the average income and the Human Development Index. Countries with a higher capacity—mainly industrialised countries—would have to support those with lower capacity;

- To what extent obligations become binding should ultimately depend on a country's contribution to climate change. The accumulated emissions since 1990 could serve as a suitable indicator. At that time, the United Nations had already identified the greenhouse effect as a human-made problem.

These rules would mean that the advanced industrialised countries, and to a somewhat lesser degree also the former planned economies, would have to take on absolute, binding reduction targets going far beyond Kyoto.

Moreover, these Annex-I-Countries would be bound to make transfer payments to the four other groups in support of climate protection. According to our proposal, the "newly industrialised countries" (NICs) and the "rapidly industrialising developing countries" (RIDCs) will also have to make an active, quantifiable contribution to reducing global emissions in the near future. The NICs could rely on rich nations co-financing some of their measures—and the RIDCs on broad funding of their climate protection by the advanced nations. Without such transfer payments, emission targets for NICs/RIDCs would not become binding. On the other hand, the remaining two groups (ODCs, LDCs) would have to gradually adopt policies and measures for a more climate-friendly direction of their development. Their burden will be to put their full efforts into adapting to climate change.

The key to the indispensable integration of the developing countries into a system of binding emission targets lies in differentiation. For this purpose, the existing country categories will have to be broken up. Even if many of the politicians of the G 77 and China negotiating group still resist the idea, there were already clear indications in Buenos Aires that the unity of the group cannot be maintained without acknowledgement of its members' heterogeneity, The countries most affected by climate change will, for example, no longer tolerate the OPEC countries blocking payments for adaptation measures with compensation demands for possibly declining oil exports.

Several other G 77 countries also gradually recognise the need to move on from the Kyoto Protocol. They are signaling willingness to negotiate. In the medium term, therefore, this group must seek unity in its multiplicity for its own sake and show concern for its own and show concern for the interests of its weaker members. Otherwise the group will lose the negotiating power required to gain necessary concessions from the advanced countries. It goes without saying that the latter have to lead the way in climate protection.

※ ※ ※

Bibliography

Books

A.C. Pigou (1960). *The Economics of Welfare,* Macmillan & Co. Ltd., London.

Ahluwalia, Montek, S. (1985). *"Rural Poverty, Agricultural Production and Prices: A Re-Examination"* in John Mellor and Desai Gunvant, M. (eds.) "Agricultural Changes and Rural Poverty," The John Hopkins University Press, London.

Amartya Sen (1995). *The Hindu,* 6th November, Interviewed by Ramamanohar Reddy, Chennai.

Betellei, A. (2000). *Chronicles of Over Time,* Penguin Books, New Delhi.

Carr, Maryn *et al.,* (1997). *Speaking Out; Women's Economic Empowerment in South Asia,* Vikas Publications, New Delhi.

Chakravarty, Sukhamoy (1989), *Development Planning, The Indian Experience,* Oxford University Press, New Delhi.

Charsely, S.R. and G.K. Karanth (1998). *Challenging Untouchability. Dalit Initiative and Experience from Karnataka,* Sage Publications, New Delhi.

Chinnadurai, K. (1986). *Evaluation Study of Implementation of IRDP,* State Bank of India, Coimbatore.

Dantwala, M.L. (1996). *Dilemmas of Growth: The Indian Experience,* Sagar Publications, New Delhi.

Delige, R. (1999). *The Untouchables of India,* Berg, New York.

Desai, B.M. and N.V. Namboodiri (1993). *Rural Financial Institutions: Promotion and Performance,* Oxford and IBH Publishing Company Pvt. Ltd., New Delhi.

Dev, S. Mahendra (1999), *State Interventions and Women's Employment,* in T.S. Papola and Alakh N. Sharma (Eds.), *Gender and Employment in India,* Vikas Publishing House Pvt. Ltd., New Delhi, pp. 373-411.

Dharm Narain & Sen, A.K. *et al.* (1989), *Studies on Indian Agriculture,* Oxford University Press, New Delhi.

Frencine Fournier (1997), *Foreword, Poverty and Participation in Civil Society.* Edited by Yogesh Atal of Else Oyen, Abhinav Publications, New Delhi.

George Psacharopoulos and Moureen Woodhall (1986). *Education for Development: An Analysis of Investment Choices,* Oxford, New York.

Griffin (1979). *The Political Economy of Agrarian Change,* The MacMillan Press Ltd., London.

Griffin Keith (1978), *International Inequality and National Poverty.* The MacMillan Press Ltd., London.

Griffin Keith (1981). *Land Concentration and Rural Poverty,* The MacMillan Press Ltd., Hong Kong.

Gunnar Myrdal (1968). *Asian Drama—An Inquiry into Poverty of Nations,* Pantheon, New York.

Gunnar Myrdal (1970). *The Challenge of World Poverty: A World Anti-Poverty Programme in Outline,* Pantheon, New York.

Gupta, D. (2000). *Interrogating Caste: Understanding Hierarchy and Difference in Indian Society,* Penguine Books, New Delhi.

Haq, Mahabub Ul (1978). *The Poverty Curtain: Choices for the Third World,* Oxford University Press, Bombay.

Haq, Mahabub Ul (1997). *Human Development in South Asia,* Oxford University Press, New York.

Harper, M. (1998). *Profit for the Poor,* Oxford and IBH Publishing Co., Delhi.

Hirway Indira (1984). *Programmes for Poverty Eradication: A Critique of Target Group Approach,* Sardar Patel Institute for Economic and Social Research (Mimeo).

Holcombe, Susan (1995). *Managing to Empower: The Grameena Bank's Experience of Poverty Alleviation,* Oxford University Press, Dhaka.

IFMR (1984). *An Economic Assessment of Poverty Eradication and Rural Unemployment Alleviation Programme and their Prospects,* Madras.

Jackson Dudley (1972). *Poverty, MacMillan Studies in Economics,* MacMillan, London.

Karmakar, K.G. (1999). *Rural Credit and Self-Help Groups, Micro-Finance Needs and Concepts in India.* Sage Publications, New Delhi.

Kaushik Dasu (1984). *The Development Economy: A Critique of Contemporary Theory.* Oxford University Press, Delhi.

Khan Azizur Rahman and Eddy Lee (1984). *Poverty in Rural Asia,* Asian Employment Programme (ARTEP), Inernational Labour Organisation, Bangkok, Thailand.

Kuznets S. (1965). *Economic Growth and Structure,* Heinemann, London.

Lewis, A. (1966). *Development Planning,* Allen and Unwin, London.

Mahammad Haan Khan (1981). *Underdevelopment and Agrarian Structure in Pakistan,* A West View Replica Edition, West View Press, U.S.A.

Maheswari, S.R. (1985), *Rural Development in India,* Sage Publications, Delhi.

Minhas, R.S. (1974). *Planning and the Poor,* S. Chand and Company Limited, New Delhi.

Mukta Mittal (1995). *Women Power in India,* Anmol Publications Pvt. Ltd., New Delhi.

Myrdal Gunner (1968). *Asian Drama,* Volume III, Twentieth Century Fund, New York.

NABARD (1999). *Banking with the Poor: Financing Self-Help Groups,* CGM, NABARD, Hyderabad.

NABARD (1999-2000), *NABARD and Micro-Finance,* Mumbai.

Nanda, Y.C. (2000). *Role of Banks in Rural Development in the New Millennium,* National Bank for Agriculture and Rural Development, Mumbai.

NCERT (2000). *Human Development in South India,* Oxford, New Delhi.

Parthasarathy, G. (1982). *Integrated Rural Development Concepts, Theoretical Base and Contradiction, in Development Planning and Policy,* Edited by Gupta D.B., *et al.,* Wiley Eastern, New Delhi.

Rahman, Hossain Zillus (1998). *Poverty Issues in Bangladesh,* Power and Participation Research Centre, Mimeo.

Rai and Tandon (1999). *Voluntary Development Organisation and Socio-Economic Development,* Indian Economic Association, 82nd Conference Volume, Amritsar.

Sakuntala Narasimhan (1999). *Empowering Women, An Alternative for Strategy from Rural India,* Sage Publications, New Delhi.

Sen A.K. (1984). *Poverty and Famines: An Essay on Entitlement and Deprivation,* Oxford University Press, Delhi.

Shylendra, H.S. (1999), *Promoting Women's Self-Help Groups: Lessons from an Action Research Project of IRMA,* Anand, India, Working Paper No. 121.

The World Bank (2000-2001). *World Development Report,* Oxford, New York.

Todaro Michael, P. (1977). *Economics for a Developing World,* Longmans, London.

Todaro Michael, P. (1990). *Economics for a Developing World,* Second Edition, Longmans, New York.

Von Braun, J., Bayes, F. and Akhter, R. (1999). *Village Pay Phones and Poverty Reduction.* ZEF Discussion Papers on Development Policy No. 18, Centre for Development Research, University of Berlin.

Von Pischke, J.D. *et al.,* (1983). *Rural Financial Markets in Developing Countries: Their Use and Abuse,* John Hopkins University, Baltimore, U.S.A.

Yogesh Atal (1996). *Poverty and Participation of Civil Society,* Abhinav Publications, New Delhi.

Zeller, Manfred and Manohar Sharma (1998). *Rural Finance and Poverty Alleviation,* Food Policy Report, International Food Policy Research Institute, Washington DC, USA.

Journals

Amitava Mukherjee (1999). *Out of the Abysis. The Challenge Confronting Some Civil Society Actors,* Indian Economic Association, 82 Conference, Amritsar.

Awasthi, P.K., *et al.,* (1986). "IRDP: Receptivity and Reaction", *Indian Journal of Agricultural Economics,* Vol. 41, No. 4, October-December.

Bagchee, Sandeep (1987). "Poverty Alleviation Programmes in Seventh Plan: An Appraisal", *Economic and Political Weekly,* Vol. XXII, No. 4, January 24.

Bardhan, P.K. (1973). "On the Incidence of Poverty in Rural India of the Sixties", *Economic and Political Weekly,* Februry.

Bhat, Mazi, P.N., *et al.,* (1999). "Finding of National Family Health Survey Regional Analysis", *Economic and Political Weekly.* Vol. XXXIV, Nos. 42 and 43. Oct. 16-22/23-29.

Chambers, Robert (1994). "Poverty and Livelihoods Whose Reality Counts?" Overview Paper II, UNDP Stockholm Roundtable, Change: Social Conflict or Harmony? 22-24 July.

Copertake, James G. (1996). *The Resilience of IRDP: Reform and Perpetuation of an Indian Myth,* Development Policy Review, 14.

Dantwala, M.L. (1983). "Rural Development: Investment Without Organisation', *Economic and Political Weekly.*

Desai, A.R. (1987). "Rural Development and Human Rights in Independent India", *Economic and Political Weekly,* Vol. XXII, No. 31.

Desai, B.M. and J.W. Mellor (1993). "Institutional Finance for Agricultural Development: An Analytical Survey of Critical Issues", *Food Policy Review I, International Food Policy Research Institute,* Washington, DC, USA.

Ghosh, D.K. (1995), *"Group Cohesiveness in DWCRA Groups: An Application of Sociometric Approach",* Kurukshetra, May-June.

Govil, R.K. (1982). "Micro-Level Planning and Rural Development", Kurukshetra.

Grewal, R.S. et al., (1985). "Impact of Integrated Rural Development Programme on Rural Women in Bhiwani District of Haryana", *Indian Journal of Agricultural Economics,* Vol. XL, No. 3, July-September.

Hara Gopal, G. & Balaramulu, Ch. "Poverty Alleviation Programmes: IRDP in an Andhra Pradesh District", *Economic and Political Weekly,* Vol. XXIV, Nos. 35 & 36, September 2-9.

Hirway Indira (1984). *Programmes for Poverty Eradication: A Critique of Target Group Approach,* Sardar Patel Institute for Economic and Social Research (Mimeo).

Jain, S.C. (1986). "Poverty Alleviation Programmes in India: Some Issues of Micro Policy", *Indian Journal of Agricultural Economics,* Vol. XLI, No. 3, Conference Number, July-September.

Karmakar, K.G. (1999). *Rural Credit and Self-Help Groups: Micro-Finance Needs and Concepts in India,* Sage Publications, New Delhi.

Kumar Rajinder, *et al.,* (1986). "Impact of Credit on Income, Employment and Capital Formulation of Rural Poor", *Indian Journal of Agricultural Economics,* Vol. 41, No. 4, October-December.

M.S. Kallur (2001). "Empowerment of Women Through NGOs: A Case Study of MYRADA Self-Help Groups", *Indian Journal of Agricultural Economics,* Vol. 56, No. 3.

Mosley, P. and R.P. Dahal (1985). "Lending to the Poorest: Early Lessons from the Small Farmers: Development Programme, Nepal", *Development Policy Review,* Vol. 3, No. 2.

NIRD (1985), "Employment and Income Generation Through IRDP, NREP and DRM", *Journal of Rural Development,* Vol. 4, No. 5, March-September.

Owusu, K. Opoku and William Tetteh (1982). "An Experiment in Agricultural Credit: The Small Farmer Group Lending Programme in Ghana", *Savings and Development,* Vol. I, No. 1.

Rajaram Das Gupta (2001). "Working and Impact of Rural Self-Help Groups and Other Forms of Micro Financing", *Indian Journal of Agricultural Economics,* Vol. 56, No. 3.

Rajasekhar, D., (1996), "Problems and Prospects of Group Lending in NGO Credit Programme in India", *Savings and Development,* Vol. 20, No. 1.

Sinha, S.P. and Prasad Jagadish (1980). 'Special Programmes for Weaker Sections: An Evaluation', *Indian Journal of Agricultural Economics,* Vol. XXXV, No. 4.

Stiglitz, J.E. (1990), "Paper Monitoring and Credit Markets", *The World Bank Economic Review,* Vol. 4, No. 3.

Thakur, D.S. (1977). "Rural Development in India: Past Experience and Tasks Ahead", *Indian Journal of Agricultural Economics,* Vol. XXXII, No. 3, July-September.

The Hindu, 11th May 2002, Chennai.

Yaron, J. (1992). *Successful Rural Finance Institutions,* World Bank Discussion Paper, 150, Washington, DC, USA.

Reports

Amitava Mukherjee (1999), *Out of the Abysis, The Challenge Confronting Some Civil Society Actors,* Indian Economic Association, 82 Conference, Amritsar.

APDPIP (2000), *On Andhra Pradesh District Poverty Initiatives Project Appraisal Document (PAD),* Report No. 20089, South Asia Regional Office.

Chief Planning Officer (2001). *Handbook of Statistics, Mahabubnagar* District, Mahabubnagar.

Chief Planning Officer Collectorate (2000). *Handbook of Statistics,* Krishna District, Machilipatnam.

Chief Planning Officer Collectorate (2001). *Handbook of Statistics,* Chittoor District, Chittoor.

CIRDAP (1998). *Increased Household Income and Rural Women in Asia, Impact on Status and Activities,* Dhaka, Bangladesh.

CIRDAP (1998). *Poverty Gender and Participation,* Dhaka.

CIRDAP (1999), *Rural Development Report, Centre on Integrated Rural Development for Asia and Pacific,* Dhaka.

CIRDAP (2000). *Poverty Gender and Participation,* Dhaka.

CMIE (2000). *Profile of Districts, Economic Intelligence Service,* October, Mumbai.

Government of Andhra Pradesh (1998). *Annual Report of the Commission of the Rural Development,* Hyderabad.

Government of Andhra Pradesh (1999). *Annual Report of the Commission of the Rural Development,* Hyderabad.

Government of Andhra Pradesh (1999). *New Series on State Domestic Product,* A.P., Hyderabad.

Government of Andhra Pradesh (2001). *Provisional Population Totals, Series 29,* Hyderabad.

Government of Andhra Pradesh (2001) *Statistical Abstract,* Hyderabad.

Government of Andhra Pradesh (2001). *Strategy Paper,* Hyderabad.

Government of India (1991). *Census of India,* New Delhi.

Government of India (1997-2002). *IX Five Year Plan,* New Delhi.

Government of India (2001). *Provisional Population Totals,* New Delhi.

Government of India (1974). *Towards Equality—Committee on the Status of Women in India.*

Government of India (1998-99). *Reports of the Commissioner of SC and STs,* New Delhi.

Haq, Mahbub Ul (1997). *Human Development in South Asia,* Oxford University Press, New York.

Holcombe, Susan (1995). *Managing to Empower, The Grameen Banks' Experience of Poverty Alleviation,* Oxford University Press, Dhaka.

IFAD (1996). *The State of World Poverty, Rome for a Discussion on the Process and Structural Causes of Poverty,* see Rovert Chambers (1983), *Rural Development, Putting the Last First,* London, Longmans, One of the Best Discussions on How These Perpetuate Poverty.

IFAD (2001). *Rural Poverty Report, The Challenge of Ending Rural Poverty,* Oxford, New York.

Indian Bank (2002-2003). *Annual Credit Plan,* Krishna District (A.P.), Vijayawada.

International Fund for Agricultural Development (IFAD) (1992). *The State World Rural Poverty—An Inquiry Into Its Causes and Consequences,* New York University Press, New York.

ISACPA (1992). *Independent South Asia Commission for Poverty Alleviation.*

NABARD (1999). *Annual Report,* Mumbai.

NABARD (2000). *Annual Report,* Mumbai.

NABARD (2001). *Annual Report,* Mumbai.

NIRD (1994). *Rural Development Report: Rural Employment,* Hyderabad, Andhra Pradesh.

NIRD (2001). *National Conference on SHG Movement in the Country and Swarnajayanti Gram Swarozgar Yojana (SGSY).* National Institute of Rural Development, Hyderabad.

PEO (1985). *Evaluation Report on Integrated Rural Development Programme,* New Delhi.

RBI (1984). *Implementation of Integrated Rural Development Programme—A Field Study.*

SAARC (1992). *The Independent Source Asian Commissions of the SAARC on Poverty Alleviation,* Dhaka.

South Asian Association for Regional Co-operation (SAARC) (1992). *Meeting the Challenge, Report of the Independent South Asian Commission on Poverty.*

The World Bank (1990). *World Development Report,* Oxford, New York.

The World Bank (1991). *Gender and Poverty in India,* Washington, DC.

The World Bank (1999-2000). *World Development Report 1999-2000,* Oxford University Press, New Delhi.

UNDP (1994). *Human Development Report,* Oxford, New York.

UNDP (1996). *Human Development Report,* Oxford, New York.

UNDP (1997). *Human Development Report,* Oxford, New York.

UNDP (2000). *Human Development Report,* Oxford, New York.

World Bank (1990). *World Development Report—Poverty,* Oxford University Press.

Yerramaraju, B. and Firdausi, A.A. (1995). *Evaluation of DWCRA in Prakasam District.* Sponsored by Government of Andhra Pradesh. Administrative Staff College of India, Hyderabad.

Others

Government of Andhra Pradesh, *Vision-2020,* Hyderabad.

Government of India (1985). *Five Year Plan Documents (The Seventh and Eighth Five Year Plans 1985-95),* New Delhi, The Planning Commission.

NABARD (1984). *Study of Implementation of IRDP (Mimeo),* Bombay.

Government of Andhra Pradesh (1999). *Vision-2020,* Hyderabad, India.

Government of Andhra Pradesh, *Guidelines for Swarnajayanti Gram Swarozgar Yojana, Panchayati Raj and Rural Development Department,* Hyderabad.

IXth Five Year Plan (1997-2000).

The Hindu (2002). April 27, Chennai.

The Hindu (2002). Vision 2020.

Index